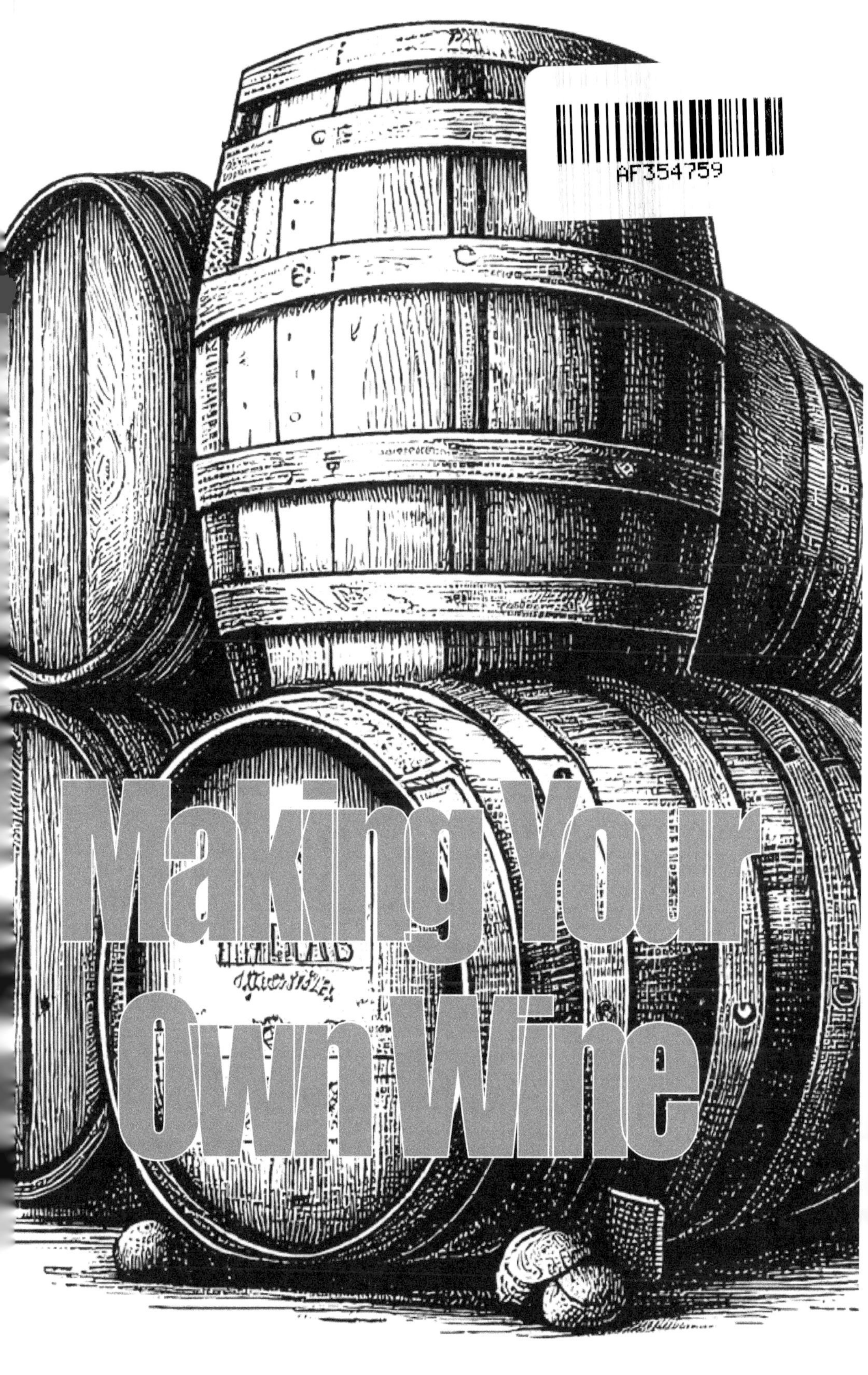
AF354759
Making Your
Own Wine

Contents

Introduction

At one time or another you must have sent away for something.
A "do it yourself kit," of some sort. Something that gave
you instructions on how to make, build, or create something.
Something that you seen, was important to you, so, you sent
away for it, and just had to do it for yourself. That's what
this electronic book is about. "The Complete Guide To Making
Your Own Wine" is a computer book, an instructional on how to
make wine. Made simple, with easy-to-understand instructions, on
how to get the job done.

It requires very little money, and very little effort. It
does require a bit of time, but this is due to the fermenting
process. When you get right down to it, everything requires
time. When was the last time you went to the bank to make a
simple withdrawl. That's time! We all know that you can't
rush aging, of any kind!

The supplies required for making wine, will be the biggest
obstacle. I have discovered that most kitchens have enough
utensils to more than "get the job done. However, there are
very few supplies that are specicialized. I have uncovered
several places that specialize in this field. They cater to
the wine makers all over the United States, and even ship
supplies abroad. So you are covered, and very well I might
ad! No wine maker has to scrounge, as in the past.

I should say that making wine is one of the most satisfying
things that you will ever achieve. Simply because its really
simple, and because time does all the grunt work for you!

STARTING INFORMATION

The simple methods described here are designed for beginners
who do not know where to begin and for those with some
experience who frequently run into difficulties and
disappointments.

The making of top-quality wines is absurdly simple, yet not
quite so simple that we can be careless about it. Too many
people are still following Granny's fruit mixtures to ferment
of their own accord, leaving bottles of fermenting wines
corked loosely (the three main causes of ruined wines), while
others are still preparing their fruits and other ingredients
in a manner which nine times out of ten produces cloudy, acid
wines that more often than not find their way down the drain.

If your previous attempts have not been up to expectations
there is a reason. This will be found with in these pages as
well as the essential, yet simple, information that ensures
success in making what is, surely, the finest home product on
Earth.

I repeatedly make it clear that I am an advocate of
simplicity. There are many highly complicated scientific and

chemical aspects underlying amateur wine-making. A few home
operators begin to dabble in these, so that, to them,
wine-making becomes a gruelling test of knowledge and skill.
Expensive laboratory equipment becomes necessary as does some
experience in laboratory techniques and from then on all
pleasures are lost in a worrying maze of technicalities. And
all for no reason at all, because their wines are no better
than those turned out by the simple methods and recipes here.
However, so that readers understand the reason for wines
being spoiled, I have included a few chemical details so that
the very beginner not only knows what to do and how to do it,
but also why he is doing it in one particular way. Success
is thus assured. Nevertheless, he will need no knowledge of
chemistry and no more in the way of utensils than is already
available in most homes.

USING UTENSILS

For making wines with the recipes and ingredients here all
one needs is a gallon-size glass bottle, an unchipped enamel
saucepan and a polythene pail. Make certain to use polythene
as some plastics are not suitable. Do not use aluminum or
copper vessels and do not use an enamel vessel not ordinarily
intended for cooking purposes as these often contain lead in
the glaze, and this could render wines poisonous.

Fermentation will not be carried out in an open vessel such
as a crock or polythene pail in all these recipes unless you
want it to; it is best to ferment the liquors in a
gallon-size glass bottle-this point will be covered again
later on. A polythene pail is necessary for only a few of
the recipes and may be disregarded for the time being.

THE ART OF FERMENTATION

This is the process by which the liquors we prepare are
turned into wine, and we have nothing to do with it. All we
do when making wine is to prepare a liquid containing
substances that will give a pleasant flavour to what will
eventually become a finished wine. The yeast we add turns

the liquid into wine for us.

Ordinarily, baker's yeast and white granulated sugar are used
by the average home wine maker. However, over the past few
years wine-making has taken such a hold that suppliers of
equipment and ingredients offer a wide range of yeasts
specially imported from the wine-producing areas of France,
Italy and Germany. These yeasts make the finest wines
because they are true wine yeasts whereas bakers' yeast in
only bread yeast and should not be expected to make good
wine-though of course it does, but not to be compared with
the results following the use of wine yeasts.

Wine yeast is capable of producing eighteen per cent of
alcohol by volume (32 proof), against the fourteen per cent
of bakers' yeast.

More and more people are using these wine yeasts together
with invert sugar instead of household sugar.

Now let us understand what happens when we add yeast to a
prepared liquor containing sugar.

Yeast is obtainable in the form of a compressed cake, dried
tablet, pellet or in power form as a liquid culture, and all
are inactive (dormant) at the time of purchase.

When making our wines fermentation is seen as a slight
frothing during the early stages and this soon settles down
to a gentle ferment that may last as long as six months. But
if warmth is given-as we shall see later on-fermentation
should be over and done with in half that time.

All the time fermentation is going on; that is, all the time
the yeast continues to reproduce itself, the amount of
alcohol in the wine increases. But it cannot go on for ever

because when what we call the maximum alcohol tolerance of
the yeast is reached, the alcohol formed kills the yeast. It
will be seen then that from the tiny amount of yeast we add
at the start masses of new yeast is made and all this helps
to make alcohol until the last surviving generation of the
original yeast is finally destroyed by the alcohol it and all
the other generations put together have formed since we
began. When this happens, fermentation ceases and no more
alcohol is made. Thus the old tale that the longer wine is
kept the stronger it becomes is proven a fallacy-or old
wives' tale.

As already mentioned, bakers' yeast can make up to fourteen per cent of alcohol by volume, while wine yeast makes from fifteen per cent to eighteen per cent by volume.

To get the maximum alcohol and to get fermentation over without undue waste of time we must keep the fermenting wine warm. The ideal temperature at which to keep a 'must' is between 65 degrees F. and 70 degrees F. However, few can manage this, but if fermenting wines are kept warm throughout fermentation time, this will do. Most people use an airing cupboard for this and it works well. Others use all sorts of ingenious devices and these are described under he heading 'Aids to Fermentation'. Do not be tempted to keep a 'must' hot during fermentation; during the warmer weather almost any warm spot in the kitchen will do, but during cold weather and especially during very cold nights it is always best if a

little added warmth can be given.

When a ferment is allowed to become cold the yeast ceases to work. This means that at some time later, if the weather

turns warm, fermentation begins again. If the wine has been bottled in the belief that fermentation has ceased for good, the result is a popping under the stairs and corks flying in

all directions and the loss of valuable wine.

FERMENTATION AIDES

Most beginners will be content to keep their fermenting wines warm in an airing cupboard or near the boiler in the kitchen. Others will want to know how they can make a special fermenting cupboard.

If only two or three jars of wine are fermenting at one time, a small cupboard with a small electric heater installed will be ideal. Alternatively, an electric light bulb hanging in a cupboard and the jars grouped round this will serve the purpose just as well, especially if the cupboard is just

large enough to accommodate the jars and not so big that a lot of warmth is lost. I know of people who group several jars round a small safety paraffin lamp, but this would only be satisfactory when the wine is under a fermentation lock

otherwise the wine might become tainted by fumes.

Other aids to satisfactory fermentation are good nutrients. Yeast nutrients, as they are called, are carefully balanced yeast foods which assist the yeast to reproduce and therefore make the largest possible amount of alcohol. Sufficient

nutrient speeds fermentation so much that, once you have used
a good one, you will always do so. I know from my vast
experience that warmth, a good yeast and good nutrient will
together make wines ten times better than any old yeast, no
nutrient and a warm atmosphere one day and a chilly one the
next. We want the best; very well, let us take just that

little extra care and spend those few extra coppers which

will make such an immense difference to the finished product.

Suppliers of special ingredients offer a variety of nutrients
are accompanied by directions how to prepare. In most cases
it is just a matter of mixing the nutrient with some of the
prepared liquor and then adding it to the brew with the
yeast.

Now, a word about 'invert' sugar. Most of you will be
content to use household sugar and it is household sugar that
I include in the recipes. However, I have proved beyond
doubt that invert sugar gives better results. this is also
obtainable from the same fires.

A summary of the foregoing is this: the inexperienced wine
maker who uses bakers' yeast, no nutrient, household sugar
and who allows the wine to ferment anywhere cannot possibly
expect the results which can be achieved by following my
advice. By doing so anyone, including beginner who do not
have to endure years of apprenticeship, with the aid of a
fermentation lock, by keeping the wine warm during the whole
of the fermenting period, using the appropriate wine yeast,
invert sugar and nutrient will obtain wines with a strength,
clarity, flavour and bouquet of which they will be justly

proud.

When bakers' yeast is used it is crumbled into the prepared
liquor. When wine yeast is used the directions supplied by
the dealer must be followed. This involves starting what is
called a 'nucleus ferment'. A half-pint mild bottle will do
for this. About a quarter-pint of water and a teaspoonful of
sugar are boiled together for a minute and then allowed to
cool. This is then put into the milk bottle-sterilized as
directed later on- and the yeast then added in whatever form
it is obtained.

The neck of the bottle is then plugged with cotton wool and
put into a warm place. Within a few days-usually three-this
little lot is fermenting merrily ready for adding to a batch

of wine that you will be waiting to make.

If you prepare the liquor for wine-making and then add the
wine yeast it will take three or four days to begin to
ferment. Better therefore to get the nucleus fermenting
ready to add to the liquor when you have prepared it so that
the whole lot is quickly in a state of vigorous fermentation.

It is most important that the yeast is not added to hot
because a temperature well below boiling will destroy the
yeast. Let the little drop of sugar-water cool well before
adding the yeast and later let the prepared liquor cool well
before adding the nucleus or 'starter bottle' as we call it.
In the recipes I shall refer to adding the yeast as 'adding
the nucleus' on the assumption that you will have taken my
advice and will be using wine yeasts prepared as directed,
but if you must use bakers' yeast merely crumble this into
the liquor at the time you would add the nucleus.

It will be seen in the recipes that all the sugar is not used
at once, this is because yeast ferments much better if the
sugar is fed to it in stages. Too much sugar at the outset
might cause the yeast to stop fermenting at around ten
percent of alcohol. Inexperienced operators might think
fermentation has finished naturally and put their wine in a
cool place to clear- which, of course it would do. But it
would be an over-sweet wine likely to start fermenting again
at any time.

For a simple re-statement; having prepared the liquor as the
recipes advise, the yeast or nucleus is added together with
the nutrient and the wine put in a warm place until all
fermentation has ceased.

In some of the recipes (chiefly those calling for flavoring
to be added at a late stage of production), directions read:
'leave until fermentation has nearly ceased'. This is rather
a broad term to beginners, but where fermentation locks are
in use they will know when this stage is reached because the
water will remain pushed up to one side of the lock and a
bubble just manages to push through every two or three
minutes.

Where fermentation locks are not in use, but where clear-
glass jars are being used, beginners will be able to see the
bubbles of gas rising. All the time there is quite a

mass of them rising steadily, fermentation is quite vigorous.
But when there is only the faintest trace of a line of
bubbles round the perimeter of the wine and where only a few
bubbles are seen rising slowly to the surface they may say,

for all intents and purposes, that fermentation has nearly
ceased-though it may go on for several more weeks.

THE CLEARING PROCESS

With the recipes and methods described here there is no need
to use isinglass or any other aids to clarifying. These
wines clear themselves usually before fermentation has
ceased. Indeed, it is usual to have a brilliantly clear wine
a month before fermentation has ceased. If one or two lots
of wine appear to be slow to clear, do not worry, a week or
two after fermentation has finally stopped clarifying will
take place very quickly. It is important to bear in mind
that a clear wine usually has a little deposit to throw, so
that it is always best to leave the wine for at least a month
after it has become crystal clear in order that the last of

the impurities an perhaps some unseen yeast cloud has time to
settle out. If this is not done, a slight sediment might
form in the bottles and when you begin to pour the wine into
a glass the sediment is churned up so that it clouds the
wine. Such a happening is not a calamity as the cloud will
settle again, probably overnight, but it means putting the
bottle away.

It is best when all fermentation has ceased, to siphon the
clear wine (if not yet crystal clear) into another jar
leaving the deposit behind. Then when the wine is finally
crystal clear it should be siphoned into bottles. This
racking, as we call it, helps to get the slight cloudiness to
settle out quickly.

NATURAL ENEMIES

The enemies of successful wine-making are wild yeasts and
acetic bacteria. The acetic bacteria which converts alcohol
into acetic acid thereby turning wine to vinegar is ever
present in the air.

Similarly, the yeasts and spores of fungi which turn wine
insipid and flat or turn it sour are also in the air. When
using fresh fruit and other ingredients from the garden or
from shops these bacteria and yeasts and fungi are already on
them, but they are easily destroyed so that they do no harm.
The ingredients we shall be using will be supplied in sealed
containers so that they will not already be contaminated by
the causes of spoilage-as we call them.

However, the water we use might contain harmful bacteria that

can spoil the wine or possibly wild yeast which can cause
what we call 'undesirable' ferments. These ferments give
'off' flavors to put it politely-otherwise sour flavors as we
refer to sourness in milk-not acid flavors.

Anyway, the methods described here ensure the destruction of
all harmful yeasts and bacteria at the outset so they need

not worry you.

Now, if wild yeasts and bacteria are in the air they must be
on corks, inside bottles and jars; indeed, they are on
everything we use. But they are easily destroyed so that
success is assured.

It is not generally known that the molds on cheese, half-
empty pots of meat paste and jam are often yeasts

growing there, and it is this kind of yeast floating about in
the air that ruins our wines if we allow it to settle. To
defeat this souring yeast we must keep our fermenting wines
and finished wines covered closely. Treatment of finished
wines is covered under the heading 'storing'. Covering
fermenting wines in jars is very simple, but most important.

Ad soon as the prepared yeast has been added to the prepared
liquid the top of the jar should be covered with a piece of
polythene. This should be pressed down all around by hand
and strong string tied tightly around. This will keep
airborne diseases away from the wine because the gas
generated during fermentation will find an outlet for itself
and keep up a constant outgoing stream, thus preventing the
diseases air contains from gaining access. Far better than
this polythene covering is a FERMENTATION LOCK.

The whole idea of fitting a fermentation lock is to prevent
air and airborne diseases reaching the wine. Firstly, the
lock is fitted to a drilled cork and the cork then fitted to

the jar. Water is then poured into the level shown. The gas
formed during fermentation pushes through the water in the
form of bubbles, but air-borne diseases are kept out. Better
than water in the lock is a little of the sterilizing
solution described latter, or a crushed and dissolved Campden
tablet. This is best because if as sometimes happens a
vacuum forms in the jar the air drawn in is purified by the
sterilizing solution. When a vacuum forms inside the jar the
lock works in reverse for a while and this often happens when
warm wine is put into a jar and the lock fitted at once. But
don't worry if this happens, because as soon as gas has been
generated the lock will begin working properly.

Another advantage of having a fermentation lock in use is
that it indicates when the fermentation has ceased.

All the time the bubbles are passing through, and all the
time the water in the lock remains pushed up to one side, it
means that there is pressure in the jar and that this
pressure is gas being formed by the act of fermentation.
When the fermentation ceases for good, the water returns to
normal. During the early stages of fermentation, bubbles are
running through the water at a rate of one a second or even
faster than this. But as fermentation slows down they become
far less frequent. Later on, the water remains pushed to one
side and it may take five or even ten minutes for sufficient
gas to make one bubble. During the very last stages of
fermentation, it may take a week for one bubble to push
through. Clearly, then, all the time the water remains
pushed up to one side the wine should be left, as it is safe
to say that fermentation is still going on.

When the water returns to normal, give the jar a vigorous
twist and the chances are that you will get fermentation on
the go again for a day or two longer. If the whole idea in
using locks is to keep airborne diseases from contaminating
the wine we must ensure that the bung and lock are airtight.
If they are not, the gas leaking will prevent air reaching
the wine during the early stages, but as it slows down the
outgoing stream of gas through the leakage holes would not be
strong enough for this so that airborne diseases could easily
reach the wine.

Having fitted the lock to the bung and jar, run a little
sealing wax round where the bungs enter the far and where the
lock enters the bung. This precaution may not be necessary,
but is is better to be on the safe side. When fermentation
has ceased the lock and bung are removed in one piece and a
new bung inserted. The wine is then put away to clear-as
mentioned before.

NOTE: I have advised sealing wax above, but candle wax does
    just as well.

Where fermentation is carried on in a polythene pail or
similar fermenting vessel during the early stages of
production, the top of the vessel should be pulled down all
around and then secured with thin strong string or a tightly
fitting elastic band. The gas generated during this early
vigorous ferment will find an outlet for itself and keep up a

constant outgoing stream so that airborne diseases cannot gain access.

<h2 style="text-align:center">STERILIZATION</h2>

As mentioned, wild yeast and bacteria are likely to be inside bottles, jars and on corks, etc. Therefore, if we are to prevent them damaging our wines they must be destroyed.

Bitter than boiling bottles, etc., in a pail of water or baking them in an oven is to use a sterilizing solution that does the job in a batter of seconds. This may be made up as follows:

Get 2 ozs. of sodium metabosulpite (or potassium metabisulphite), there being two forms. Nearly fill a half-gallon bottle with warm water and then add the crystals (or powder) and revolve the far until all is dissolved. Try

to use a glass stoppered jar or bottle for this.

To sterilize bottles and jars with this, pour a pint into the first bottle and shake it up so that all the inside is wetted. Then pour it into the next bottle and so on and then back to the bulk again. Having treated the bottles, it is best to rinse them out with boiled water that has cooled well. This will rid the bottles of the rather pungent odor of the sterilizing solution. But don't worry id a slight whiff remains in the bottles, because it will do no harm. Having rinsed the bottles, let them drain for a minute or two and they are now ready for use.

Corks. More wine has been ruined through using unsterilized corks than through any other cause. The crevices of corks teem with all sorts of harmful bacteria and spoilage yeasts.

The best way to sterilize them is to put them in a small basin with something heavy on top to keep them submerged-a heavy cup will do-and then cover with the sterilizing solution. Leave this for about ten minutes and during the time you are bottling a batch of wine. As each cork is required, take it, dip it in boiled water and then wipe it dry with a cloth dipped in the sterilizing solution-which, incidentally, is known as sulphur dioxide or sulphite solution.

The drying of corks is necessary to prevent the weight of the wine pushing our the corks when the bottles are put away on their sides.

<h2 style="text-align:center">SIPHON, BOTTLING & HOW TO STORE</h2>

It is almost impossible to pour clear wine from one bottle to another without stirring up the lees (deposit). the best method is to siphon the clear wine at bottling time.

First, put the bottle or jar of wine on a table and the empty bottles on a box or stool on the floor. Then, using a yard and a half of surgical rubber or plastic tubing, siphoning is quite a simple operation. Put one end of the tubing in the full jar (or the first of the full bottles) and suck the

other end until the wine comes. As soon as this happens, pinch the tube at your lips and, while holding on tightly, put this end in the first empty bottle and let the wine flow. As the empty bottle nearly fills, slowly press the tube between finger and thumb in order to cur off the flow slowly rather than with a jerk. Sudden stoppage often stirs up the deposit. When the bottle has filled to the shoulders pinch the tube at the neck of the bottle being filled and put this end into the next bottle and let the wine flow again.

As the level in the full jar falls, lower the tube into the wine. But be careful not to lower so far that the deposit

begins to be sucked into the tubing. A good way of avoiding this is to ask a chemist to let you have fifteen inches of quarter-inch tubing and get him to bend the last inch of one end upwards. Then fit the straight end to the rubber tubing you have. At siphoning time, insert the glass tube to the bottom of the full jar of wine. The bend in the tube will rest on the bottom of the jar, but the opening of the end bent upwards will remain above the lees.

Now let me give the impatient wine-maker a warning. I know how nice it is to build up a stock and build it quickly, but don't be in such a hurry that you put wines away that are not yet perfectly clear. This results in disappointment upon opening if, as often happens, you decide to try a bottle of the oldest and the best you have for some special friend and find that you have stirred up a deposit and clouded what you imagined to be a perfectly clear wine. A reliable test to decide whether a wine is perfectly clear or not-and one I always carry out before bottling for storage purposes-is to hold a high-powered torch against the bottle. If there is no

suggestion of a beam passing through a hase, then the wine is as clear as you will get it; but if there is a slight beam of light, leave the wine to clear perfectly. You will soon get used to this little test and be saved from what might be a most embarrassing position.

Finally, when the clear wine has been bottled and the corks have been rammed home they should be sliced off level with the rim of the bottles. Sealing wax should then be run over the whole surface and the bottles stored on their sides.

Sealing and storing in this fashion is important because it allows for the wine to keep the cork moist and so prevent shrinkage. Shrinkage would cause cracking in the sealing wax with the result that tiny air holes would appear through

which wild yeast and bacteria can attack the wine.

In the ordinary way a well-made wine-that is one made with good yeast and nutrient-is strong enough in alcohol to preserve itself. A goodly percentage of alcohol acts as its own preservative and that of the wine itself. But poorly made wines are low in alcohol and can be spoiled in the bottles if air reaches them. Our wine, made by the recipes and directions here, will contain enough alcohol to destroy any wild yeast or bacteria that might reach it owing to shrinkage of corks. Nevertheless, it is still important that air is not allowed to reach the wine, because if it did so for prolonged periods the quality would deteriorate, the flavor suffer and much of the bouquet be lost.

Experienced wine makers -- myself included -- use the new plastic seals which when fitted to a bottle of wine shrink tightly, effecting a perfect airtight seal. I expect you have come across these often enough on bottles of cordial. The T'Noirot extracts described in later chapters are fitted with these. When these capsules (as they are called) are used the bottles may be stored upright. Storing bottles horizontally often presents a problem for some people, but friends of mine with a small cupboard to spare have lined it with orange boxes. In each partition they have fitted

soft-drink cardboard crates so that each orange box holds twenty-four bottles on their sides. Having heard that wines must be stored at a temperature which should remain constant throughout the year, people are going to all sorts of trouble and thinking up all sorts of ingenious devices to achieve that end. Opinion is divided as to the ideal temperature in which to store wines-probably because wines, like human beings, prefer what suits them individually. The temperature suitable for one wine is not necessarily best for another.

Rapid changes of temperature are certainly best avoided, so if you can store your wines on a stone floor or in a cupboard which has a stone floor, so much the better. If you cannot do this, store your wines where you can and don't worry.

MATURING

I am afraid I always have to suppress a grin when people ask
me how long a wine needs to mature because I know that all
they really want to know is how soon they can drink it. It

is surprising the number of people who simply will not
believe that wines improve with age. They set about making
wines possessed of urgency which should not exist and an
impatience that is hard to believe. They really believe that
wine can be made, matured and drunk in six or seven weeks.
With luck, you might get fermentation over and done with and
your wines clear and bottled in that time, and truly they are
drinkable even so young, but-and it is an enormous 'but'-wine
tasted at that tender age cannot be compared with the same
wine tasted a year later. It is impossible to describe the
changes that take place, but take place they do. Chemical
changes are taking place constantly, so that one batch of
wine does not taste the same when sampled at intervals of six
weeks.

I know full well that you will be itching to get your teeth
into these wines and I cannot blame you for that -- I'm the
same myself, always anxious to sample the latest batch to be
bottled off. And it is a waste of time for me to tell you to
keep it at least a year before drinking because I know you'll
never manage it; especially after you had a taste of it when
siphoning it into bottles.

But please do this for your own sake. At bottling time, put,
say, two bottles in the attic or some place where they cannot
be reached easily-send them to me if you like. Seriously,
those two bottles of each lot made will soon amount up to a
nice little stock. The remaining four bottles from each
gallon may be used as required.

The whole secret of building up a stock is to make several
lots at the same time and when a jar is emptied at bottling
time, start again with another lot. In this way you will
always have a few gallons fermenting, several dozen bottles
for use as required and a dozen or so slowly growing into a
nice reserve. Then, when the first two bottles put away are
a year or two old you may sample them. These will have
become such magnificent wines in that time that your lesson
will have been well and truly learned and the vow taken that
hence forth half of all that is bottled is going to the

attic. I hope it does, and I hope even more that you will be

able to keep some of it for five years at least. For at five

years it is better than age four and at three years old it is
better than age two. I have proved all this to myself and
have a few bottles of wine that I made over fifteen years
ago.

BRIEF, BUT IMPORTANT

FERMENTATION LOCKS:

There is no substitute for the fermentation lock, although
many people use a balloon stretched over the jar instead of a
fermentation lock, and provided this is a tight fit, it will
certainly protect the wine. But this cannot give any
indication as to when fermentation has ceased. The Balloon
is fitted over the neck and, as gas escapes into it, slight
inflation takes place and as pressure grows the gas forced
out round the neck of the jar.
Another substitute for the lock is a three-inch piece of
quarter-inch bore glass tubing stuffed with cotton wool and
fitted in the same way as the lock. But, as with a balloon
this can give no indication as to when fermentation has
ceased.

YEAST-AND ADDING IT:
It will be seen in the recipes that I give 'yeast' without
mentioning any kind. This is because some of you will be
using bakers' yeast and others one of the many varieties of
wine yeast. In the directions which accompany the recipes
the time to add the yeast is clearly stated. If bakers'
yeast is used, use half an ounce and crumble this into the
jar at the time advised. Experienced wine makers and those
using wine yeasts for the first time will have their little
nucleus ferments ready and these will be added at the time
advised in the directions given with each recipe.

SUGAR WATER (Syrup):
In the recipes and directions it will be seen that the sugar
and water are added to the mixtures as a syrup. Make sure
the sugar has dissolved before the water comes to the boil.
And so that mistakes do not occur, label the jar so that you
know how much sugar has to be added at each stage. There is
no need to be exact when adding 'one third' or whatever the
direction happens to be, but it is a good plan to have the
total amount of sugar to be used at the outset put aside; in
this way, when all has been added you will know there is noo
more to go in and you will not be left wondering if you have
used as much as you should have done.

GALLON JARS:

Someone is sure to ask before they begin: How can I get a
gallon of water, the flavoring, and all that sugar into a

one-gallon jar? The fact is that, in the way we shall be
doing it, it is quite a simple mater. Gallon jars hold half
a pint more than a gallon when full, and because we shall be
adding the sugar in stages, most of each lot of sugar will be
used up before the next is added. Before the last lot of
sugar and water is added, the wine is transferred to another
jar and the deposit thrown away. This will leave space for
the last lot of syrup to be added. If, through some
misfortune, this is not quite the case, put the little
remaining syrup in a freshly sterilized screw-stoppered
bottle and screw down tightly. This will keep it save for
the few days necessary for fermentation to reduce the liquor
in the jar and so make room for that little drop of
left-over.

If at the time called for in the recipes you do not have a
second jar in which to put the fermenting wine (at the time
given for disposing of the deposit) you may pour the wine
into any suitable container, then throw away the deposit,
clean out the jar, sterilize it and then return the wine to

it.

SAUCEPANS:
If it happens that your saucepans are not quite large enough
to hold the sugar and five pints of water that is to be
boiled at the first stage of making the wine, boil the sugar
in a quart of water and the remaining three pints of water in

another saucepan then mix.

FRESH FRUIT WINES

There is no need for me to mention the enormous popularity
this branch of home wine-making enjoys, or that countless
thousands of people all over the world embark with tremendous
enthusiasm each summer upon turning wild fruits and surplus
garden fruits into wines fit to grace the tables of a
banqueting hall. Just let me say that, no matter how
advanced methods become and how easily obtainable special
ingredients for wine making are, there will always be in the
hearts of everyone a place for the true country wines, for
they have that indefinable 'something' which sets them apart
from all others, a uniqueness that cannot be found in any
other wine either commercial or home produced.

The methods I use myself are described here, and although

they are the simplest and the surest ever evolved, it is
necessary to point out the complications that arise if these
methods are not used.

Years ago-and, I am very sorry to say, even today-many
thousands of unfortunate home wine makers are following
methods which advocate: 'crush the fruit, add the water and
leave to ferment'. Other methods advise boiling the fruits.
In both cases disappointment is almost a certainty, and the
reason for this is easy enough to understand.

The gray-white bloom that forms on grapes and other fruits is
yeast put there by nature and it may be said that the first
wine known to early man was the result of this yeast
fermenting fruits crushed for a purpose other than
wine-making. In the ordinary way, this yeast might well make
good wine if allowed to ferment alone. Unfortunately with
this yeast comes what we term 'undersiable' yeast (wild
yeast), and several kinds of bacteria-each of which can ruin
our wines. They bring about what we call 'undersiable'
ferments that usually take place at the same time as the
ferment we want to take place so that instead of a wine of
quality the result is one tasting of flat beer or cloudy
evil-smelling liquid fit only for disposal. Another
bacterium, known as the vinegar bacterium, will turn wines
into vinegar.

Since there is nothing we can do when any of these calamities
has occurred, they must be prevented from happening.

Clearly, we must destroy all these enemies before beginning.
The simplest method is of course-at first thought anyway-is
to boil the fruits. But here rises another problem. All
fruits contain pectin, a glutinous substance which causes
jams to 'set'. Boiling fruit releases pectin. This pectin
holds itself and minute solids in suspension. Giving the
wine a cloudiness that is impossible to clarify or even
filter out. We may put the crushed fruit through a jelly-bag
to remove every particle of pectin-bearing fruit and then
boil the juice only, but this is a messy, tedious job that

takes hours and eliminates all the pleasure from wine-making.

Obviously, what we need is a method which will destroy the
wild yeast and bacteria on the fruits (as boiling does)
without actually boiling, and, indeed, without heating our
fruits at all because it needs very little heat to bring out

the pectin.

Our method, known as the 'sulphiting' method, does just this and produces full-bodied, crystal-clear wines easily and quickly without fuss or bother. All that is necessary to achieve this are tablets costing just pennies. Campden fruit-preserving tablets are available in bottles of twenty from most chemist. In the ordinary way-and provided the fruit is not too heavily affected with wild yeast and bacteria-one tablet will destroy the undesirable element contained in one gallon of crushed bruit pulp, but we cannot be sure of this. Now, two tablets will surely do this, but being a comparatively heavy dose this might also destroy the yeast we shall be adding so that the ferment we desire does not take place. My method takes care of both these risks, not only destroying the wild yeast and bacteria on the

fruits, but also allowing the yeast we add to ferment alone and unhindered to produce wines of clarity and quality the like of which cannot be produced by any other method. By adding one Campden tablet to a good deal less than one gallon of fruit pulp ('must') this will represent a rough equivalent to two tablets per gallon. But before we add our yeasts we shall have increased the amount of liquid or pulp to nearly twice the amount, consequently reducing the amount of sterilizing solution to half or the equivalent of one Campden tablet per gallon. In this way we achieve our overall aim.

Each Campden fruit-preserving tablet contains four grains of sodium metabisulphite; therefore, any readers finding Campden tablets in short supply may ask their chemist for four grains

of sodium metabisluphite (or potassium metabisulphite-there being two forms), and use this. But because a chemist would find a single order of four grains rather trivial, it would be best to ask for say, six or ten packets each containing four grains. If you are making two-gallon lots of wine the amount to use would be eight grains. Do not be tempted to buy by the ounce and measure out a grain as this is impossible unless you have the appropriate scales.

Just in case you happen to be one of those people who, even in these enlightened days, abhors the use of chemicals, let

me assure you that sulphur dioxide (the solution which results when Campden tablets are dissolved) is quite harmless to humans when used in the proportions recommended. Indeed, as many as eight tablets (thirty two grains) may be used with safety, but such heavy dosing would prevent a 'must' fermenting.

The sulphiting method is used by the trade, so we shall be following a method well tried and proved.

Heaven knows how many hundreds of gallons of wines I have made by this method and all with the same unfailing success.

Method 1 makes wines of the heaver type; their flavors are more pronounced and their color more full than those produced by method 2. Those wishing for lighter wines more suitable for serving with meals should use method 2. The main difference in the two methods is that we ferment the fruit pulp itself in method 1, and the juice only in method 2. It will be appreciated that when fermenting the pulp we must as a matter of course get far more from our fruits. But we do not want too much in a light wine otherwise the subtle difference between a heavier wine and the popular lighter wines is lost.

The short pulp ferment of method 1 ensures that we get all the flavour and desirable chemical matter from our fruits in the right proportion.

The best method to use for each type of fruit is given with each recipe. It should be taken into account that varied amounts of fruit and sugar with the use of proper method produce distinctly different types of wine.

METHOD 1:
Crush the fruit by hand in a polythene pail and pour on one quart of boiled water that has cooled. Mix well. Crush one campden tablet and dissolve the power in about half an egg cupful of warm water and mix this with the fruit pulp. Leave the mixture for one or two hours. A little bleaching will take place but this is nothing to worry about.
After this, take one-third of the sugar to be used (or approximately one-third) and boil this for one minute in three pints of water. Allow this syrup to cool and then stir into the pulp. Then add the yeast (or nucleus) and ferment for seven days.
After seven days, strain the pulp through fine muslin or other similar material and wring out as dry as you can. Put the strained wine into a gallon jar and throw the pulp away. Then boil another one-third of the sugar in one pint of water for one minute and when this has cooled add it to the rest. Plug the neck of the jar with cotton wool or fit a fermentation lock and continue to ferment in a warm place for a further ten days.
At this stage, if you have not a spare jar, pour the wine into a polythene pail leaving as much of the deposit in the jar as you can. Clean out the jar, sterilize it and return

the wine to this.

The remaining one-third of the sugar may now be boiled for
one minute in the remaining pint of water. When this has
cooled, add it to the rest. Refit the lock or plug the neck
of the jar with fresh cotton wool. After this, the wine
should be left in a warm place until all fermentation has
ceased.

NOTE: If there is not quite enough space for all of this last
lot of syrup, put the remainder in a sterilized
screw-top bottle and store for a few days in a cool
place. This may be added when fermentation has reduced
the level of the liquid in the jar. If you have to do
this, don't forget to refit the lock.

METHOD 2:

Crush the fruit in a polythene pail and add one quart of
boiled water that has cooled. Mix well.

Crush one Campden tablet and dissolve the powder in about
half an egg cupful of warm water and mix this with the fruit
pulp. Leave the mixture in a cool place for twenty-four
hours, stirring twice during that time. Strain through fine
muslin or other similar material and squeeze gently but not
too hard. Discard the fruit pulp.

Then boil one-third of the sugar in half a gallon of water
for one minute and allow to cool. Mix this with the juice
and return the lot to the polythene pail. Then add the yeast
(or nucleus), and ferment for ten days.

After this, pour the top wine into a gallon jar leaving as
much of the deposit behind as you can. Boil another
one-third of the sugar in half a pint of water for one minute
and when it is cool add it to the rest. Plug the neck of the
jar with cotton wool or fit a fermentation lock and ferment
in a warm place for fourteen days.

After this, boil the remaining sugar in the remaining
half-pint of water for one minute and when cool add it to the
rest. refit the lock or plug the neck of the jar with fresh
cotton wool and leave in a warm place until all fermentation
has ceased.

The recipes are designed to make one gallon of wine, it two
gallons are being made at once twice the amount of each
ingredient must be used (including Campden tablets) and the
sugar and water added in double quantities. This principle
applies where three or four gallons are being made and it is
easy enough to work out. Just to be sure that mistakes do
not occur when adding the syrup-sugar and water-stick a label
on the jar and note on this the amount added.

Readers will be quick to appreciate that certain fruits are
more suitable than others for making certain types of wine.

Clearly, it would be as hopeless to try to make port from
rhubarb as it would be to try to grow potatoes on a pear
tree, and I think it is in this respect that many people go
astray; they make wines from the cheapest and most readily
available fruits (naturally enough) but they do not give the
slightest thought to what the result will be or whether they
will like it or not. Before you begin decide on the type of
wine you are most likely to prefer and then use the fruit and
the method which will make this type of wine.
Elderberries make an excellent port-style wine and many
variations, each with the basic port style underlying them,
so that from this lowly wild fruit we may obtain not only a
full-bodied port-style wine, but also a Burgundy style, a
claret and others according to the whim of the operator.
Blackberries make similar wines, as do certain varieties of
plumbs, damsons and black currants. The juice from
lighter-colored fruit such as raspberries, loganberries, red
and white currants and others make excellent table wines.
But there is no need to cover this aspect fully here because
every recipe is preceded by the name of the type or style of

wine that can be expected from each recipe. I say 'expected'
because to guarantee that the wine will be identical to the
one expected would be unwise, but only because the amounts of
sugar and acid present in the fruits vary from season to
season-indeed, they vary with the type of tree, soil,
situation and with the sort of summer we have had while the
fruits have been growing. A hot summer produces fruits
containing more sugar and less acid than a wet sunless
summer, when the effect is the reverse.
In each recipe appears the name of the best yeast to use and
this is best added as a nucleus as already described. If you
must 'use bakers' yeast or a dried yeast, merely sprinkle it
over the surface of the 'must' at the time given in the
method you are using.

A final word. Make sure all fruits are ripe. This is far
more important than most people imagine. Half-ripe fruits or
those with green patches on them should be discarded as it
needs only one or two of these to give a gallon of wine an
acid bite. Fully ripe fruit is essential if we hope to make
the best wine.

When we have decided that our garden fruits are ripe enough
or those you have your eye on in the hedgerows, leave them
for another three or four days before gathering.

RECIPES 1 - 32 (BERRY WINES)

1. BLACKBERRY WINE (Port Style):
   4lb. blackberries, 4lb. sugar (or 5lb. invert), 7pts.
   water, port yeast, nutrient.
   Use method 1. Ferment the pulp.

2. BLACKBERRY AND ELDERBERRY WINE (Port Style):
   2 1/2lb. elderberries, 2 1/2lb. blackberries, 7pts. water,
   3 1/2lb. sugar (or 4lb. invert), port yeast, nutrient.
   Use method 1. Ferment the pulp after crushing and mixing
   together.

3. BLACKBERRY WINE (Burgundy Style):
   4-5lb. blackberries, 3 3/8lb. sugar (or 4lb. invert),
   burgundy yeast, nutrient, 7pts water.
   Use method 1. Ferment the pulp.

4. BLACKBERRY WINE (Beaujolais Style):
   This recipe was passed on to me by a friend. It won 1st
   prize among 600 entries on the occasion of the 2nd
   National Conference and Show for Amateur Wine-Makers at
   Bournemouth. Unfortunately it wasn't my orginial recipe,
   or I could have won that prize!
   4 1/2lb. blackberries, 2 1/2lb. sugar (or 3lb. 2oz.
   invert), burgundy yeast, nutrient, 7pts. water.
   Method 1 was used. The wine was, of course, dry.

5. BLACKBERRY WINE (Light Table Wine):
   3lb. blackberries, 3lb. sugar (3 3/4lb. invert), 7pts.
   water, burgundy yeast, nutrient.
   Use method 2. Ferment the diluted juice.

6. BLACKCURRANT WINE (Port Style):
   4lb. blackcurrants, 1lb. raisins, 3lb. sugar (or 3 3/4lb.
   invert), port yeast, nutrient.
   Use method 1. Ferment the pulp with the raisins.

7. BLACKCURRANT WINE (Port Style):
   4lb. blackcurrants, 7pts. water, 3 1/2lb. sugar (or 4lb.
   invert), port yeast, nutrient.
   Use method 1. Ferment the pulp.

8. BLACKCURRANT CLARET:
   3lb. blackcurrants, 2 1/2lb. sugar (or 3lb. invert), 7pts.
   water, all purpose wine yeast, nutrient.
   Use method 2. Ferment the diluted juice.

9. BLACKCURRANT WINE (A Light, Sweet Wine):
   3 3/4lb. blackcurrants, 3 1/2lb. sugar (or 4lb. invert),

7pts. water, al-purpose wine yeast, nutrient.
Use method 2. Ferment the diluted juice.

10. CHERRY WINE (A Delightful Sweet Wine):
8lb. black cherries, 7pts. water, 3 1/2lb. sugar (or 4lb.
invert), all-purpose wine yeast or Bordeaux yeast,
nutrient.

Use method 1 Weight with stones and ferment the pulp.

11. CHERRY WINE (A Light Dry Wine):
8lb. black cherries, 7pts. water, 2 1/2lb. sugar (or 3
1/4lb. invert), sherry yeast is best, otherwise
all-purpose wine yeast, nutrient.
Use method 2. Ferment the strained diluted juice.

12. REDCURRANT WINE (Light Table Wine):
3lb. redcurrants, 7pts. water, 3lb. sugar, (or 3 3/4lb.
invert), all-purpose wine yeast, nutrient.
Use method 2. Ferment the strained diluted juice.

13. REDCURRANT WINE (A Light Medium-Sweet Wine):
4lb. redcurrants, 7pts. water, 3 1/2lb. sugar (or 4lb.
invert), all-purpose wine yeast, nutrient.

Use method 2. Ferment the strained diluted juice.

14. DAMSON WINE (Port Style):
8lb. damsons, 7pts. water, 4lb. sugar, (or 5lb. invert),
port yeast, nutrient.
Use method 1. Weight with the stones and ferment the
pulp.

15. DAMSON WINE:
Suitable for making into Damson Gin-See 'Recent
Experiments'.
5lb. damsons, 7pts. water, 3lb. sugar (or 3 3/4lb.
invert), all-purpose wine yeast, nutrient.
Use method 1. Weight with the stones. Ferment the pulp.

16. DAMSON AND ELDERBERRY WINE (Port Style):
3lb. damsons, 1 1/2lb. elderberries, 3 1/2lb. sugar (or
4lb. invert), port yeast, nutrient, 7pts. water.
Use method 1. Ferment the pulp.

17. DAMSON AND DRIED PRUNE WINE (Burgundy Style):
Prunes should be soaked overnight, the water discarded
and the prunes added in the crushed state to the crushed
damson.

4lb. damsons, 2lb. dried prunes, 7pts. water, 3lb. sugar,

(or 3 3/4lb. invert), burgundy yeast, nutrient.
Use method 1. Ferment the crushed pulp.

18. RASBERRY WINE (Light, Dry):
4lb. rasberries, 2 1/2lb. sugar, (or 3lb. 2oz. invert),
7pts. water, sherry yeast or all-purpose wine yeast,
nutrient.
Use method 2. Ferment the strained diluted juice.

19. RASBERRY WINE (Sweet Dessert):
4lb. rasberries, 1lb. raisins, 7pts. water, 3 1/2lb.
sugar, (or 4lb. invert), all-purpose wine yeast and
nutrient.
Use method 2. Ferment the strained diluted juice but with
the chopped raisins for the first seven days.

20. ELDERBERRY WINE (Port Style):
4lb. elderberries, 7pts. water, 4lb. sugar (or 5lb.
invert), port yeast, nutrient.
Use method 1. Ferment the crushed pulp.

21. ELDERBERRY WINE (Medium Dry):
3 1/2lb. elderberries, 3lb. sugar (or 3 3/4lb. invert),
7pts water, sherry yeast or all-purpose wine yeast,
nutrient.
Use method 2. Ferment the strained diluted juice.

22. ELDERBERRY CLARET (Dry, of course):
3lb. elderberries, 2 1/2lb. sugar (or 3lb. invert), 7pts.
water, sherry yeast or all purpose wine yeast, nutrient.
Use method 2. Ferment the strained diluted juice.

23. PLUM WINE (Burgundy Style):
8lb. plums, any fully ripe variety is suitable, 7pts.
water, 3lb. sugar (or 3 3/4lb. invert), burgundy yeast,
nutrient.
Use method 1. Weight with the stones and ferment the
crushed pulp.

24. PLUM WINE (Port Style):
Dark red, fully ripe fruits must be used. 10lb. plums,
7pts. water, 3 1/2lb. sugar (or 4lb. invert), port yeast,
nutrient.
Weight with the stones. Use method 1. Ferment the crushed
pulp.

25. RHUBARB WINE:
This wine is best made on the dry side and used as an

appetizer. If you try to make it sweet, it would have to
be rather too sweet. Four pounds of sugar will make it a
medium sweet wine, but even this will not reduce the
acidity which gives this wine its character which,
unfortunately, is causing it to lose its popularity. It
is possible to remove the acid by using precipitated
chalk, but this is hardly for beginners and a practice
which, in any case, alters the whole flavour of the
resulting wine.
5lb. rhubarb, 3lb. sugar (or 3 3/4lb. invert), 7pts.
water, sherry yeast or all purpose wine yeast, nutrient.
Crush the rhubarb with a rolling pin, starting in the
middle of each stick. Soak for five days in three pints
of water (boiled), and in which one Campden tablet has
been dissolved.
Then strain, wring out dry and warm just enough to
dissolve half the sugar.
Having done this, ferment for ten days and then proceed
as you would with any other recipe here, adding the rest
of the sugar and water in stages.

26.   LOGANBERRY WINE:
   3 to 4lb. loganberries, 3lb. sugar (or 3 3/4lb. invert),
   burgundy yeast, nutrient, 7pts water.
   Use method 1. Ferment the crushed pulp.

27.   GOOSEBERRY WINE (Table Wine:)
   6lb. gooseberries, 3 1/2lb. sugar (or 4 1/4lb. invert),
   7pts. water, tokay yeast or all purpose wine yeast,
   nutrient.
   Use method 1. But ferment pulp for three days.

28.   GOOSEBERRY WINE (Sherry Style):
   The best gooseberries for this wine are those that have
   been left on the bushes to turn red or yellow, according
   to variety. They should be firm but soft and at the same
   time not damaged. Any damaged ones and any with a
   suggestion of mould or mildew on them must be discarded.
   For a dry sherry style use 2 1/2lb. sugar, for a medium
   dry use 3lb., and for a medium sweet use 3 1/2lb., or the
   corresponding amounts of invert sugar.
   5lb. gooseberries, 7pts. water, sugar (as above), sherry
   yeast or all purpose wine yeast, nutrient.
   Use method 1. But ferment the pulp for five days only.

29.   WHORTLEBERRY WINE (Burgundy Style):
   Whortleberries are a small wild fruit which many people
   come to the country to pick; they make excellent jams and

jellies-and very good wines, otherwise known as 'herts'.
6pts whortleberries, 7pts. water, 3lb. sugar(or 3 3/4lb.
invert), burgundy yeast, nutrient.

Use method 1. Ferment the pulp.

30.   WHORTLEBERRY WINE (Port Style):
8pts. whortleberries, 7pts. water 4lb. sugar (or 5lb.
invert), port yeast, nutrient.
Use method 1. Ferment the pulp.

31. WHORTLEBERRY WINE (Table Wine):
5pts. whortleberries, 7pts. water, 2 1/2lb. sugar (or
3lb. 2oz. invert), all purpose wine yeast, nutrient.
Use method 2. Ferment the strained diluted juice.

32.   SLOE WINE:
Sloes make a delightful wine which is very popular with
those living in the country, and is particularly suitable
for turning into sloe gin. Not more than 4 lb. should be
used owing to their astringency.
4lb. sloes, 3lb. sugar (or 3 3/4lb invert), 7pts. water,
all purpose wine yeast, nutrient.
Use method 1. But ferment pulp for three days only.

RIBENA WINE TUTORIAL

Before I explain how easy it is to make wine with ribena let
me point out that this famous syrup of excellent quality
could well be added to fermenting 'musts' made up from of the
fruits to get special results. The rate to add it would be

one to two bottles per gallon.

When making wines from dried fruits the addition of one or
two bottles of Ribena per gallon would make a vast
improvement to the flavour and quality of the wine.

Similarly, when making wines from fresh fruits that give a
red wine, one or two bottles or Ribena could well be added to
make up for other fruits in this wy, you mar disregard the
SO2 preservative (more about this later) because the amount
in the Ribena will not be enough to stop fermentation, but it
would be best to add it at the vigorous fermentation

stage-during the first ten days.

If you propose to use Ribena in this way, bear in mid that
each bottle contains approximately eight ounces of sugar, so
you should reduce accordingly the amount of sugar in

whichever recipes you are using.

Undiluted Ribena is not readily fermentable, because it contains just over seven pounds of sugar per gallon and is preserved with 350 parts per million SO_2-either of which is capable of preventing fermentation.

Obviously, our aim when making wine with Ribena will be to reduce the amount of sugar to about three and a half pounds per gallon, by using half Ribena and half water. In doing this, we shall reduce the SO_2 preservative to around 175 parts per million. This amount is unlikely to prevent fermentation, though it could do so.

My trials with ribena were carried out with the above point borne in mind and it will be seen that I began with a good deal less than equal parts or Ribena and water, gradually bringing them up to equal parts.

Because I did not want to overwork the yeast by giving it too much sugar to work on at the start, and because I wanted to reduce the SO_2 content to below 175 parts per million (without heating with the risk of spoiling the flavor of the syrup), I decided to work to the following method. The method, incidentally, met with the approval of V. L. S. Charley, B.BC., PH.D., technical director of the Royal

Foresty factory of the Beecham group and one-time director of the Long Ashton Research Station, Bristo.

All water used in the process was first boiled and allowed to cool naturally.

STAGE 1:
Two bottles of Ribena were diluted with twice the amount of water (four Ribena bottles full). Yeast in the form of a nucleus was added and the mixture allowed to ferment for ten days.

STAGE 2:
After ten days' fermentation, two bottles of ribena and one Ribena bottle of water were added and the mixture allowed to ferment for a further ten days.

STAGE 3:
After a total of twenty days' fermentation, two bottles of Ribena and one more bottle of water were added. Fermentation was then allowed to carry on to completion, taking, in all, three months.

The result was a good, round wine flavored delightfully but not too strongly of fresh blackcurrants.

At stage 3 it was borne in mind that, while most of the SO2 would have been driven off during fermentation by adding those last two bottles, I was, in effect, bringing the total SO2 content up to 175 parts per million. fearing that the yeast might be just a little weakened at this stage I decided to drive off the SO2 in the last two bottles by raising the temperature of the to 70 deg. C. If you want to do this and have no suitable thermometer, stand the bottles in a saucepan of water and slowly raise the temperature until the Ribena in the bottles has increased in volume enough to reach the rims of the bottles. The temperature is high enough to drive off the SO2 and the heat should be cut off at once. The caps of the bottles must be removed before heating. The whole of fermentation was carried out in narrow-necked bottles plugged with cotton wool, fermentation locks being fitted after ten days. Racking was not carried out until one month after the last addition. Monthly racking followed until fermentation ceased. Even at this early stage the wine was nice to drink, but it had improved vastly at the age of six months.

At first it might seem expensive to make wine with Ribena, but against the cost one should set the fact that no sugar need be added and that one has a top-quality product all ready for the job in hand. Apart from this, there is no expensive fruit to buy, no messy crushing-in fact nothing much to do at all. And, most important of all, Ribena has been treated with a pectin-destroying enzyme, which means that you could boil it if you wished without fear of pectin clouding the finished wines. Such boiling would, of course, drive off the SO2 and give you a wine flavored slightly to cooked blackcurrants.

It will be seen that a sweeter wine may be made by using one bottle more of Ribena or one less of water, while a dry wine would result if less Ribena were used. A dry wine would lack the fuller flavour, but this would be offset to some extent by to dryness.

If eight bottles of Ribena are made into one gallon by adding water, the gallon will contain roughly four pounds of sugar and the equivalent of four pounds of blackcurrants. This amount of fruit is ample for a gallon of wine and, provided one likes a fairly sweet wine, this proportion of sugar to fruit is not too much. On the whole, I feel that seven bottles of Ribena would be the limit you could use to make a gallon of wine without it being too sweet.

It will be clear that my trials with Ribena, using six
bottles to make just under a gallon of wine, have been most
successful and I do urge readers to have a go.

A point to bear in mind is that a good light wine is often
made with as little as two pounds of blackcurrants to the
gallon, therefore, if you made four bottles of Ribena into a
gallon of 'must', you would have used the equivalent of two

pounds of blackcurrants and two pounds of sugar. This would
give you a wine of about twelve percent of alcohol by volume.
Such a wine would be dry, but by adding half a pound of sugar
during the process you would get a sweeter wine of one or two
percent more alcohol.

EXTRACT TUTORIAL

This chapter shows how easily wines the flavor of world
famous liqueurs and other commercial products may be added
with the minimum of utensils and labor; indeed, this is
probably, if not decidedly, the simplest the least

troublesome and the most rewarding of all adventures into
wine-making.

In what are known as T'Noirot Extracts we have a readily
prepared ingredient and, as will be seen in the recipes, no
preparation is needed, the stuff is ready to use.

You might get a decent imported wine or British wine at seven
and six a bottle, but you will never be able to buy wines
with the flavour of these world-famous liqueurs at any price,
and certainly not for thirty cents a bottle-all they will
cost you to make. Nor will you ever buy Vermouth at less
than fifty cents a bottle; the Vermouth recipe alone,

then, must be worth a fortune to anybody who likes Vermouth.

When making these wines do please use good yeast and
nutrient, for the results obtained in this way will surpass
any you can hope to achieve by using bakers' yeast and no
nutrient.

It will be seen in the recipes that I have included invert
sugar because this gives the best results here. Invert sugar
contains a little acid and this is essential in wine-making
as we have already seen. If you use household sugar, you
will have to add the juice of one lemon or one-eighth ounce
of citric acid to give just the tiny amount of acid required.

When adding the extract to the prepared syrup (sugar-water),
make sure you get all of it out of the bottles.

When deciding which extract to use, you must first decide on
which you are likely to prefer (unless you know in advance
and from experience that you like Vermouth or Kirsh or cherry
brandy) and then choose that one. In this way you will make
a wine that might disappoint you-after all, not all tastes

are the same.

VERY IMPORTANT: The method we shall be using calls for adding
        these very highly concentrated flavorings to
        a very small amount of liquid to begin with.
        The flavor will be very, very strong, so do
        not sample it, and the odor given off might
        strike people as not quite pleasant. This is
        quite natural, so do not be put off using
        them because of this. And don't take a
        'sniff' of the wine during the early stages,
        for the same reason.

T'NOIROT EXTRACTS AND WHAT THEY ARE MADE OF

The following list contains the names of most of the T'Noirot
Extracts that we shall be using in this chapter and beside
each appears details of their contents. The extracts are
scientifically blended to give flavors identical to the

world-famous liqueurs of the same names. Thus you are

assured of the real thing and not a synthetic substitute.

These flavorings are highly concentrated and should not,
therefore, be judged by their odor. Anyone smelling the raw
undiluted material or sampling the wines made from the
extracts is likely to imagine that something is not quite
right. Do not pay any attention to the strength or pungency

of the odor and do not sample any wines being made from the
extract until fermentation has almost ceased. Even at this
stage it is not wise to try to judge the wine. Wait, I
implore you, until fermentation has ceased altogether and the
wine has been clear for at least a month. As with all other
wines, the flavor improves immensely with age. I am able to
speak from first-hand experience because I have been making
wines with these extracts, and I can assure you in absolute
sincerity that each extract makes a wine identical in flavor
to the world-famous commercial liqueur the name of which it
carries.

And let me just add that the oil of juniper mentioned in
other parts of this book is an extract of juniper

berries-juniper being an ornamental shrub grown a good deal
in this country.

LIQUEUR GREEN CONVENT
LIQUEUR YELLOW CONVENT
Both distilled from plants growing in the high mountain
regions. These two established the now world-wide reputation
of T'Noirot.

CURACAO, RED
CURACAO, WHITE
Two liqueurs of Dutch origin distilled from small green
oranges.

CHERRY BRANDY

Made from unfermented cherries.

DANZIG

A liqueur of German origin.

KUMMEL
Of continental origin, extracted from caraway seed. Wine
made from this extract would act as a stimulant of the
digestive organs.

MARABELLE

Distilled from the famous Lorraine plum.

PRUNELLE

Distilled from the wild plum.

Many of the extracts contain blends of bitter and aromatic
plants-Vermouth being a good example of this. We are all
well aware of the delicate flavors of the French and Italian
Vermouths and will thus be enabled to appreciate the value of
all the T'Noirot Extracts, for they bring us something quite
unique when it comes to making wines from them.

These extracts were not intended for the purpose to which I
put them. Making wines from them instead of fruit or other
ingredients is my own idea entirely and I am proud to be the
originator of both the idea and of the recipes herein. I am
also proud to pass them on to my readers all over the world.

As will be seen in the recipes, I have advised carrying out
the entire fermentation in the gallon jar, but if you would

prefer to ferment for the first ten days in a polythene pail
by all means do so, but make certain it is covered as
directed earlier. If you do this, give the liquor a good
stir before putting it into the jar otherwise some of the
deposit and a lot of flavoring may be lost. Do not on any
account divide the liquor, say, into two half-gallon lots

because half-gallon jars happen to be available. Keep it as
one until all fermentation has ceased. When this has
happened the clearer wine may be siphoned off the deposit
into another jar and put away to clear. When clear, it
should be bottled.

WINES FROM CITRUS FRUITS
(Make these Wines with Bakers' Yeast-Fresh)

61. ORANGE WINE:

This is a delightful wine that develops a flavor that can
readily be likened to an orange-flavored whisky.
12 large oranges, or their equivalent, 4 lb. sugar, 1/2
oz. yeast, 1 gal. water, nutrient.
Drop the whole oranges into boiling water, and push each
one under the surface. Then take them out and throw the
water away.
Cut the oranges into small pieces and pour over them half
a gallon of boiled water that has cooled. Cover well,
and leave to soak for forty-eight hours, crushing and
pressing the peel between the fingers to extract the oil
which gives a very special flavour. Then boil half the
sugar in a quart of water for two minutes and when cooled
add this to the orange pulp. Then add the yeast and
nutrient. Ferment this in a warm place for five days.
Then crush, strain through fine muslin or other suitable
material and wring out dry. Discard the pulp and return
the fermenting liquor to the fermenting vessel, and allow
to ferment for a further ten days. Carefully pour off
into a gallon jar, leaving as much of the deposit behind
as you can.
Then boil the rest of the water and sugar together and
when cool add to the rest. Then fit fermentation lock or
cover as directed and continue to ferment in a warm place
until all fermentation has ceased.

62. LEMON WINE:

This wine is not ordinarily mad to drink as a wine. It
is often made by experienced wine makers for blending
with dried fruit wines which sometimes fall short of acid
requirement. But more often it is made as a novelty. It

is particularly suitable for making into lemon gin wine.
Use the above directions for making orange wine-using
eight lemons instead of using oranges.

63. GRAPEFRUIT WINE:

This is another acid wine, but many people like it,
especially where a pound of raisins or dates are
fermented with the grapefruits.
Use eight large grapefruits following the orange wine
recipe above. If you wish to add a pound of raisins or
dates do so as soon as you have cutup the grapefruits and
ferment them with the rest for the first few days-until
straining time.
NOTE: If raisins or dates are used, use half a pound less
of sugar, because dried fruits contain approximately
fifty percent sugar.

64. TANGERINE WINE:

This makes a really delightful wine and a many tangerines
may be used as suits you-but do not use less than fifteen
or more then thirty.
Dates or raisins may be used with this as well as in the
grapefruit recipe and the notes about this should be
followed if you want to add them. However, I feel that
you would find the raw fruits more to your liking.
Follow the directions for orange wine when making
tangerine wine.

FLOWER WINES AND MISCELLANEOUS RECIPES

Let me begin this chapter by assuring you that one of the
loveliest wines I have ever tasted was made with gorse
flowers by a member of the Bourneouth Wine-Makers' Circle.

This I sampled while lecturing at the Town Hall there on the
occasion of the Amateur Wine-Makers' Second Annual Conference
and Show.

Flower wines, cannot, of course, be likened to any other
homemade wine-or commercial wine-because their flavors are
unique; they can only be described as delicately aromatic,
their bouquet cannot be found in any other wine.

Their popularity is lessened only by the labor of collecting
the flowers; but by choosing a spot where they abound, enough
for a gallon or two may be gathered in an hour.

Care is needed if we are to get the best from our

ingredients. When gathering the flowers it is best to use a
basket of ample size because crushing will damage the flowers
and we shall not get such a delightful wine.

All flowers should be gathered on a dry day but not
necessarily on a sunny one; though it must be sunny when
collecting dandelions otherwise they are either closed or
half-closed and difficult to find. In their closed state
they teem with insects which would get into the wine and
spoil it. Dandelions close when gathered but this does not
matter. In fact it is a great help because we should use
only the petals of dandelions, and when they are closed the
petals may be pulled out all together merely by holding the
head of the flower and pulling on the petals grouped
together.

Although only petals should be used many people make quite
good dandelion wine by using the whole heads, but I use
petals only.

To achieve the best result a wine yeast should be used and
this may be an all-purpose wine yeast. Invert sugar should
not be used in these recipes because it is inclined to
slightly alter the aroma of the flower and change the
delicate color of the wines made from recipes in this
chapter.

Bakers' yeast is included in the recipe together with
household sugar; those preferring to use a wine yeast
'started' as directed may, of course, do so.

65. GORSE WINE:
   5 pts. gorse flowers, 3 lb. sugar, 1 gal. water, 1 oz.
   yeast, Five pints is the minimum amount of gorse flowers
   to use, you may use more if you wish-up to one gallon if
   you can get them. Other ingredients would remain the
   same.
   Put the flowers in the fermenting vessel and pour on half
   a gallon of boiling water. Cover and leave to soak for
   three days, stirring each day and covering again at once.
   Boil half the sugar in a quart of water for two minutes
   and when this is cool add the flower mixture. Then add
   the yeast and ferment for three days.
   Strain out the flowers and continue to ferment the liquor
   in the fermenting vessel for a further seven days.
   Then pour into a gallon jar, leaving as much of the
   deposit behind as you can. Boil the rest of the sugar in
   the remaining water for two minutes and when cool add to

the rest. Cover as directed or fit fermentation lock and□
continue to ferment until all fermentation has ceased.
NOTE: Many people prefer this when the juice of one lemon
is added at the same time as the yeast.

66. CLOVER WINE (Use only Mauve Clover):
   3 qts. clover heads, 2 lemons, 3 lb. sugar, 1 gal. water,
   1 oz. yeast.
   Pull off the petals by gathering them between the fingers
   whilst holding the base of the flower head. Put the
   petals in the fermenting vessel and pour on half a gallon
   of boiling water. Leave well covered for twelve hours.
   Boil half the sugar in a quart of water for two minutes
   and when cool add this to the rest. Then add the yeast
   and ferment the mixture for seven days.
   Strain our the flowers, but do not squeeze to hard, and
   put the liquor into a gallon jar. Then boil the rest of
   the sugar in the remaining water and when cool add this
   to the rest. Cover or fit fermentation lock and leave
   until all fermentation has ceased.

67. DANDELION WINE:
   1 gal. flower heads with the tiniest piece of stalk, 3
   lb. sugar, 1 oz. yeast, 1 gal. water, 2 lemons.
   Remove petals as directed for clover wine. Put the
   petals in the fermenting vessel and pour on three quarts
   of water-boiling and leave to soak for seven days, well
   covered.
   Stir daily, and cover again at once. Stain and wring out
   fairly tightly and return the liquor to the fermenting
   vessel. Boil half the sugar in a pint of water and when
   cool add to the liquor, then add the yeast and the juice
   of two lemons.
   Cover as directed and ferment for seven days. Then pour
   carefully into a gallon jar, leaving as mush deposit
   behind as you can. After this, boil the rest of the
   sugar in the remaining pint of water and when cool add to
   the rest. Cover as directed or fit fermentation lock and
   leave until all fermentation has ceased.

68. COLTSFOOT WINE:
   1 gal. coltsfoot flower, 3 lb. sugar, 1 gal. water, 1 oz.
   yeast.
   Pull the petals off in the same way as for dandelions.
   The method for making this wine is identical to the
   recipe for making dandelion wine.

69. HAWTHORN BLOSSOM WINE:

2 qts. of the flower, 3 1/2 lb. sugar, 1 oz. yeast and 1
gal. water.

Gathered when the are about to drop they may be shaken
off into the fermenting vessel.
The method for making this wine is identical to the
recipe for making dandelion wine.

70. ELDER FLOWER WINE:

1 gal. flower, 1 gal. water, 3 1/2 lb. sugar, 1 oz.
yeast, 2 lemons.
Boil half the sugar in half a gallon of water and while
boiling pour over the flowers in the fermenting vessel.
Add the juice of the lemons and when the mixture is cool
add the yeast. Cover as directed and ferment for seven
days.
Strain out the flowers and wring out well, but not too
dry. Put the strained liquor in a gallon jar.
Boil the rest of the sugar and water for two minutes and
when cool add to the rest. Cover as directed or fit
fermentation lock and leave until all fermentation has
ceased.
Another very good elder flower wine may be made in
exactly the same way as the above using only five pints
of the flowers with three pounds of sugar, two lemons, 1
oz. yeast and one gallon water.

71. ROSE PETAL WINE:

One of the most delightful of all flower wines. The
petals of roses of various colors may be used in one lot
of wine, but if you have enough of, say, both red and
yellow for a separate lot of each, do keep them separate.
3 qts. rose petals (strongly scented if possible), 1 gal.
water, 3 lb. sugar, 1 oz. yeast, 2 lemons.
Pour half a gallon of boiling water over the petals in
the fermenting vessel, cover well and leave for
forty-eight hours, stirring often.
Boil half the sugar in a quart of water for two minutes
and when this is cool add to the petal mixture and
ferment for three days.
Strain and wring out well, and return the liquor to the
fermenting vessel and let it ferment for a further ten
days.
Pour the liquor into a gallon jar, leaving as much of the
deposit behind as you can. Then boil the rest of the
sugar and water as before and when cool add to the rest
together with the juice of the lemons. Cover again as
directed or fit fermentation lock and leave until all
fermentation has ceased.

72. TEA WINE:

Many wine-makers save left-overs from the teapot until
they have enough to make a gallon of wine, but I find
that the flavour of the wine is somewhat impaired when
this is done. Better to make a gallon of weak tea and to
start straight off. Don't be tempted to make strong tea
for this purpose otherwise you will have too much tannin
in the wine.
8 teaspoonsful of tea, 1 gal. water, 1 lb. raisins, juice
of 2 lemons, 3 lb. sugar, 1 oz. yeast.
Make tea in the ordinary way using eight teaspoonfuls and
a quart of water. Let it stand undisturbed for ten
minutes, and then strain into the fermenting vessel.
Boil half the sugar in half a gallon of water for two
minutes and when cool add this to the tea. Then add the
raisins and finely sliced lemons and their juice. Add
the yeast and ferment for ten days, stirring daily.
Strain into a gallon jar. Then boil the rest of the
sugar in the remainder of the water for two minutes and
when cool add this to the rest. Cover as directed or fit
fermentation lock and leave to ferment in a warm place
until all fermentation has ceased.□

73. IMITATION TIA MARIA:

I am not fond of this myself, but I know of a good many
people who are and who make this wine quite regularly.
The best plan is to make either easy potato wine or easy□
parsnip wine, and when this has ceased fermenting flavor
it with freshly made coffee or one of the proprietary
brands of essence. But do this very carefully as it is
easy to overdo it, thus spoiling the flavour.

74. ROSE HIP WINE:

One of the finest of all home-made wines; its flavour is
unique and it has body and bouquet that take a lot of
matching. Rose hips abound in early autumn and it
matters not whether they are gathered from your own rose
trees or from the hedgerows. They should not be used
until they have taken on their winter coat or red or
orange according to the type.
4 lb. rose hips, 3 lb. sugar, 1 gal. water, 1 oz. yeast.
Wash the hips well in half a gallon of water in which one
Campden tablet has been dissolved. Crush the hips with a
mallet or chop them. Put them in the fermenting vessel
and pour on half a gallon of boiling water. Boil half
the sugar in a quart of water for two minutes and when
cooled a little add to the rest. Add the yeast and

ferment the pulp for seven days.
Then strain out the solids and put the strained liquor
into a gallon jar. Boil the rest of the sugar in the
remaining water for two minutes and allow to cool well
before adding to the rest. Cover as directed or fit
fermentation lock and leave to ferment in a warm place
until all fermentation has ceased.

WINES FROM DRIED HERBS

In case the advantages of making wines from dried herbs do
not immediately become evident, let me explain that the town
and city dweller (and countryman, too, for that matter) may
make all the old favourite wines of Granny's day for next to
nothing. Practically no work is involved because, unlike
fresh fruits which have to be gathered and roots that have to
be scrubbed, grated and boiled, suitable packets of herbs are
available ready to use. In cases, many town and city
dwellers might well know of the old country wines and wish
that they could make them- indeed, they may well have lived
in the country and tasted the wines made from the fresh
herbs; dandelion, sage, coltsfoot, mint, balm, yarrow, and
countless others.

People living in large towns like Coventry and Birmingham
have written to me asking about this field of winemaking, for
they recall their early days when 'Mum' used to make what
they now describe as 'really wonderful wines form leaves she
used to collect from the fields all round where we used to
live'.

Dried herbs normally cost less than twenty cents per packet
and such a packet is usually more than enough for a gallon of
wine. The actual amount of the dried article may be varied
according to personal tastes, but usually two ounces is
enough for one gallon, and this amount rarely costs very
much. I have found that the packets of herbs supplied by
Heath and Heather Ltd., of St. Albans, Hertfordshire
(branches in many towns), are usually suitable for one gallon
of wine-though the amount in each packet varies slightly with
the variety of herb.

Those who know their herbs well enough to gather them fresh
from the garden or field or hedgerow may do so, of course,
but it must be borne in mind that one needs at least one
pound of the fresh plant to get the equivalent of two ounces
of the dried. It is most important on should be expert at
identification because many health-giving herbs bear a

striking resemblance to others which have proved themselves
to be deadly poisonous. By buying ready packeted herbs such
risks are done away with, and Health and Heather Ltd. will
send to anyone free on application their book of herbs.

In some of the recipes which follow the addition of raisins
or wheat, or both, is recommended, while I would stress that
their use is quite optional, I do strongly advise readers to

use them where they are specified unless they know in advance
that they prefer wines made without them. The use of raisins
or wheat, or both, adds body and bouquet where these
properties may be lacking. As you will have guessed, theo
herb gives only flavour-apart from its known medicinal
properties-and some aroma, but does not give the same amount
of bouquet as a fully flavored fruit; wheat and raisins help
in this respect. As with root wines, the addition of acid is
necessary an this way may be added as citric acid at the rate
of a quarter-ounce per gallon or as the juice of two large
lemons-whichever suits you best.

A nutrient is also necessary for the same reasons as have
already been described early in this book.

The amounts of sugar in the recipes are those generally used,
but readers now know that they make their herb wines dry
merely by reducing the amount of sugar according to their
wishes.

It should be borne in mind that while we use a gallon of
water, and while the sugar, occupies space at the rate of a
quart to every four pounds, we shall arrive back at the
gallon of wine aimed at because there will be some loss
during boiling, lost of most of the sugar which will be
fermented out and some small wastage when transferring to
other bottles. A little less sugar is use in these recipes
as compared with fresh fruit wines; this is because there is
no acidity or astringency to balance, as is often the case
where fruit wines are made.

The amount of herbs given in the recipes are the amounts
usually used and I advise readers to use them to begin with.

Later, say when fermentation has nearly ceased, they may
sample for strength of flavour; if they feel they would like
it stronger, a little more of the herb may be added, but this
should not be necessary.

On the other hand, if the flavour happens to be a little too

strong a pint or two or boiled and cooled water may be added
to dilute the strength or flavor. This will increase the

overall amount of wine so that the amount of sugar added will
not be enough for the increased amount. Therefore, when
boiling the additional water, with it three to four ounces of
sugar to each pint and then add this syrup slowly, taking
samples until the strength of flavour is right. The recipes
in this chapter have been given to me by friends. The trials
I have carried out with them have proven most satisfactory
and I know readers will be pleased with the results. As will
be seen most recipes call for two ounces of herb, but it will
be found that the one-and-sixpenny packets of dried herbs
from Health and Heather will suffice in all but exceptional
cases, where, for example, a very strong flavour is required.
Where Kola nuts are used, a tenpenny packet is enough.

All dried herbs may be obtained from most chemists, but
sometimes their stock is likely to be a little old. Health
and Heather deal in this field to such a large extent that
their herbs can be relied upon to give the best results.
Alternatively get them from a reliable herbalist if you have
one in your locality.

The following method is suitable for all recipes in this
chapter.

Lemons and oranges should be peeled, the fruit broken up and
added and the peel discarded.

METHOD: Put all the ingredients (except sugar and yeast) in a
        polythene pail and pour on half a gallon of boiling
        water, leave for two or three hours covered as
        directed. Then boil half the sugar in a quart or
        water or two minutes and add this to the rest while
        still boiling. Mix well, and when cool enough add
        the yeast and nutrient. Cover again and ferment in a
        pail in a warm place for ten days, stirring daily and
        covering again at once.

        After ten days, strain out the solids and wring out
        as dry as you can, and put the strained liquor into a
        gallon glass bottle. Boil the other half of the
        sugar in the remaining quart of water for two
        minutes. When cool add this to the rest. Cover as
        directed or fit with a fermentation lock and continue
        to ferment in a warm place until all fermentation has
        ceased.

75. BALM WINE:

2 oz. dried balm leaves, 2 lemons, 3 lb. sugar, 1 gal.
water, yeast and nutrient.

76. PARSLEY

WINE:

2 oz. dried parsley, 1 oz. dried mint, (or 1/2 oz., fresh
mint), 1/2 oz. dried sage (red), 1 gal. water, 2 oranges,
2 lemons, 3 lb. sugar, (or 3 3/4 lb. invert), yeast and
nutrient.

77. BROOM

WINE:

2 oz. dried broom flowers, 2 lemons, 1 lb. raisins, 2 1/2
lb. sugar (or 3 1/4 lb. invert), yeast and nutrient.

78. DAMIKOLA

WINE:

2 oz. dried damiana leaves, 1 oz. kola nuts, 1/2 oz.
dried red sage, 1 lb. raisins, 3 lb. sugar (or 3 3/4 lb.
invert), 2 lemons, 1 gal. water, yeast and nutrient.

79. SAGE

WINE:

3 oz. dried sage, 1 lb. raisins, 1 oz. dried mint, 1 lb.
wheat, 2 lemons, 2 1/2 lb. sugar (or 3 1/4 lb. invert),
yeast and nutrient, 1 gal. water.

80. YARROW

WINE:

2 to 3 oz. of dried yarrow flowers, 2 lemons, 2 oranges,
3 lb. sugar (or 3 3/4 lb. invert), 1 gal. water, yeast
nutrient.

81. CLARY

WINE:

3 to 4 oz. clary flowers, 1 lb. raisins, 2 lemons, 3 lb.
sugar (or 3 3/4 lb. invert), 1 gal. water, yeast and
nutrient.

82. BURNET

WINE:

3 oz. burnet herb, 1 lb. raisins, 1 lb. wheat, 2 oranges,
2 lemons, 3 lb. sugar (or 3 3/4 lb. invert), 1 gal.
water, yeast and nutrient.

I do strongly advise you to experiment with half gallon lots
of these and to add tiny amounts of aniseed or liquorice as
fermentation nears completion. If you do this with varying

amounts of herbs you must not let the total weight of the
herbs exceed four ounces to the gallon of wine being made. I
realize, of course, that a beginner cannot have any definite
plan for blending because he will not be familiar with the
flavors given to the wines by the various herbs. If you
accidentally spoil the flavour of a wine by trying to improve
it, you may dilute with sugar-water, and while fermentation

is still going on, add other herbs to the the flavour you are
aiming at. If you happen to find that the flavour is not□
quite strong enough you may suspend a bag of herbs in the
fermenting 'must' until you get the strength of flavour you
want. And this may be tested at few-day intervals by
tasting.

No matter how many years you may have been making wines and
no matter how many different varieties you have made, it will
be clear from the number of recipes in this book that there
are plenty you have not tried your hand at. However, do not
be tempted to make thirty or forty different varieties on a
grand scale. Make, say, half a dozen build lots with recipes
and fruit you are familiar with, and experiment with half
gallon lots. In this way you will always have a nice stock
and if any particular experiment goes wrong or perhaps does
not turn out quite as hoped, little will be lost.

WINES FROM DRIED FRUITS AND GRAIN

The making of wines from grain and dried fruits is a boom to
the townsman who finds these ingredients easily obtainable
and they make good wines. Mixtures of dried fruit and grains
make for strong, fully flavored, but not too fully flavored
wines which, when not made too sweet, are often likened to
whiskeys and brandies. They need time to mature or reach
their best-two years is not too long, though at one year old
they are very excellent wines. As with root wines the
addition of some acid is necessary here (see root wines), and
this is put into the 'must' in the form of oranges and

lemons.

Most dried fruit is heavily sulphited to prevent
fermentation, and most wheat or other grain has been in
contact with all sorts of dirt, dust and bacteria. Therefore
they must be well cleansed before use. Break up the raisins
and drop them into boiling water. As soon as the water boils
again cut off the heat, strain the raisins and throw the

water away. The raisins are then ready to use. Do the same
with wheat or other grain, but use a separate saucepan; they
are then ready to use.

TANNIN:
Most recipes for fruit wines allow for tannin in the fruits
to be given into the 'must'. This tannin forms an important
part of the flavour of the wine-though few people realize it.
But they soon know when there is too much because the wine
takes on the flavour or 'tang' of strong unsweetened tea.

The little tannin given to fruit wines is usually just the
right amount.

In the ordinary way there is no tannin present in dried
fruitwines. Therefore it is as well to add one tablespoonful
of freshly made tea-not too strong-to make good this
deficiency. Special grape tannin is available, but tea is a
cheap and handy source of which we might as well make use.
The addition of tea is included in the recipes.

83. CANADIAN WHISKY:
 2 lb. wheat, 2 lb. raisins, 1 lemon, 4 oranges, 3 lb.
 sugar, 1 oz. yeast, 5 qts. water, 1 tablespoonful of
 freshly made tea.
 Boil half the water with half the sugar for one minute
 and then pour on the wheat and raisins. Put the lot into
 the fermenting vessel and squeeze in the juice of the
 lemon. Cut up the oranges and their peel and put these
 with the rest. Work the orange peel between the fingers
 to press out the oil-much flavour is obtained form this.
 When cool add the yeast and ferment for ten days. Then
 strain out the solids and wring out as dry as you can and
 put the strained liquor into a gallon jar with a
 tablespoonful of freshly made tea.
 Boil the rest of the sugar and water of one minute and
 when this is cool add to the rest. Cover as directed or
 fit fermentation lock and leave until all fermentation
 has ceased.

84. BRAVERY'S OWN SCOTCH:
 This is another recipe that has become well known amongst
 wine makers throughout the country.
 1 1/2 lb. wheat, 1 1/2 lb. raisins, 4 oranges, 3 1/2 lb.
 sugar, 1 oz. yeast, 9 pts. water, and 1 tablespoonful of
 freshly made strong tea.
 Prepare the wheat raisins as already advised and put them
 in the fermenting vessel with the sliced oranges and
 their peel.
 Boil half the sugar in three quarts of water for two
 minutes and pour this over the material in the fermenting
 vessel. Mix well and when cool add the yeast. Cover as
 directed and ferment for seven days, stirring well each
 day and covering again at once. Strain and wring out dry
 and put the strained liquor into a gallon jar with the
 tea. Then boil the rest of the sugar in the remaining
 three pints of water for two minutes and when cool add to
 the rest. Cover again as directed or fit fermentation
 lock and leave until all fermentation has ceased.

85. RAISIN WINE:

3 lb. raisins, 3 lemons, 2 lb. sugar, 9 pts. water, 1 oz.
yeast, 1 tablespoonful of freshly made tea.
Less sugar than usual is required here because the large
amount of raisins will give a lot of sugar to the
wine -- which will not be dry. For a dry raisin wine use
only one and a quarter pound of sugar.
Put the raisins and the sliced lemons and the tea in the
fermenting vessel. Boil all the sugar in all the water
(or half the water at a time if your saucepan is on the
small side), and add the rest while boiling. When cool,
add the yeast and ferment for fourteen days, stirring
daily and covering again at once.
Strain and wring out as dry as you can and put the
strained liquor into a gallon jar. Cover as directed or
fit fermentation lock and leave until all fermentation
has ceased.

86. PRUNE PORT:

6 lb. prunes, 2 lemons, 3 1/2 lb. sugar, 9 pts. water, 1
oz. yeast. (no tea in this one.)
Wash the prunes in water in which one Campden tablet has
been dissolved and put them in the fermenting vessel.
Boil two pounds sugar in seven pints water and pour over
the fruit while boiling. Allow to cool and add the
yeast. Cover and ferment for ten days, crushing well
each day as soon as the fruit has become soft.
After ten days, crush well and strain out the solids.
Wring out as dry as you can and put the strained liquor
in a gallon jar.
Boil the rest of the sugar in the remaining two pints of
water and when cool add the the rest. Cover as directed
or fit fermentation lock and leave until all fermentation
has ceased.

87. CURRANT WINE:

No lemons are required here as currants contain
sufficient acid, neither is tea required.
4 lb. currants, 1 lb. raisins, 2 3/4 lb. sugar, 1 oz.
yeast, 9 pts. water.
Prepare the currants by the method given for prunes in
the previous recipe, and put in the fermenting vessel.
Boil half the sugar (or roughly half) in seven pints
water for two minutes and pour on to the currants at
once. Allow to cool and add the yeast. Cover as
directed and ferment for twelve days, crushing and
covering again each day.

After twelve days, strain out the solids and wring out as
dry as you can and put the strained liquor into a gallon
jar.
Boil the rest of the sugar in the remaining two pints of
water for two minutes and when cool add to the rest.
Cover as directed or fit fermentation lock and leave
until all fermentation has ceased.

88. DRIED APRICOT WINE:

This is a really delightful pale gold wine that most
people like as a dry wine. See 'Low-Alcohol Wines for
the Ladies'.
6 lb. dried apricots, w oranges, 3 1/2 lb. sugar, 9 pts.
water, 1 oz. yeast, 1 tablespoonful of freshly made tea.
Put the apricots in the fermenting vessel with the cut-up
oranges and their peel. Fold the orange peel and squeeze
to get as much oil out of it as you can.□
Boil two pounds of sugar in seven pints of water for two
minutes and pour over the fruits while still boiling.
Allow to cool and add the yeast. Cover as directed and
ferment for ten days, crushing by hand each day and
covering again at once.
After ten days, strain and wring out as dry as you can an
put the strained liquor in the gallon jar. Boil the
remaining sugar in the last two pints of water for two
minutes and when cool add to the rest, and then add the
tea. Cover as directed or fit fermentation lock and
leave until all fermentation has ceased.

89. DATE WINE:

This wine has very little flavour of its own, therefore
lemons and oranges must be added to give a nice flavour,
and the amount of oranges here will make it into a lovely
wine.
However, if you want a wine of little flavour for some
special purpose, say, blending with one that has too much
flavor or for flavoring as you wish with an extract or
whatever you may have in mind, use no oranges at all.
3 lb. of packeted or loose dates, 1 lemons, 6 oranges
(see note), 2 lb. sugar, 9 pts. water, 1 oz. yeast 1
tablespoonful of freshly made tea.
The method of preparing ingredients and for making this
wine is identical to that given in the recipe for making
dried apricot wine.

90. PRUNE AND RAISIN VINTAGE:

3 lb. prunes, 1 lb. raisins, 1 lb. wheat, 2 lemons, 2
oranges, 3 lb. sugar, 9 pts. water, 1 oz. yeast.

Prepare the raisins, prunes and wheat as has already been
advised and put them with the sliced oranges and lemons
in the fermenting vessel.
Boil half the sugar in seven pints water for two minutes
and pour over the ingredients while still boiling. Allow
to cool and add the yeast.

Cover as directed and ferment the mixture for ten days,
crushing well each day and stirring up the wheat and□
covering again at once.
After ten days, strain out the solids, and wring out as
dry as you can and put the strained liquor in a gallon
jar. Boil the rest of the sugar in the remaining two
pints of water and when cool add to the rest. Cover as
directed or fit fermentation lock and leave until all

fermentation has ceased.

91. IRISH WHISKEY:

2 lb. wheat, 1 lb. raisins, 1 lb. potatoes, 2 lemons, 4
oranges, 1 oz. yeast, 3 lb. sugar, 9 pts. water.
Prepare the wheat and raisins as has already been
directed and put them in the fermenting vessel with the
sliced lemons and oranges.
Scrub, grate and boil the potatoes in five pints of water
for not more than ten minutes, taking off all scum that
rises. Boil gently for a little longer if scum still
rises at the end of ten minutes until no more scum
rises-taking off every bit of it.
Strain this hot liquid over the ingredients in the
fermenting vessel and throw the potatoes away. Then boil
half the sugar in two pints of water for two minutes and
add to the rest. Allow to cool, add the yeast and
ferment the mixture ten days covered as directed.
After ten days, strain and wring out dry and put the
strained liquor into a gallon glass jar. Boil the rest
of the sugar in the remaining two pints of water and when
cool add this to the rest. Cover as directed or fit
fermentation lock and leave until all fermentation has
ceased.

NOTE: Imaginative readers will be quick to notice that varied
amounts of ingredients make very different types of
wines and they may wonder whether they can invent a
recipe to suit themselves. They can. Almost any
recipe in this chapter may be varied to suit individual
tastes, or it may be modified and other ingredients or
flavorings added. Take care when altering recipes not
to use too much of any particular kind so that your
overall amount of ingredients would exceed six pounds,

otherwise the wine will be spoiled.

WINES FROM GRAPES

In the ordinary way, recipes for wines made entirely from grapes are not a practicable proposition. This is because grapes are merely crushed and fermented without either sugar or water being added. Provided you have enough grapes, making wines from them is the simplest winemaking of all-that is, of course, provided they are fully ripe. Small unpruned bunches often contain a lot of small undeveloped fruits between the large juicy ones and these must be removed before the bunches are crushed. The whole bunches, stalk as well, are used as these add something to the wine. The yeast forming the bloom on your grapes may be the kind that will make excellent wine, but we cannot be sure of this owing to the near-certainty that wild yeast and bacteria are present with it. As we have seen in previous chapters, we must destroy these yeasts and bacteria and add yeasts of our choice to make the wine for us.

You will need at least twenty pounds of grapes to be assured of a gallon of wine-and this amount may not make one gallon of wine, though it make make one gallon of strained 'must'. Therefore the more grapes you have the better.

If enough grapes are available, the process is as follows:

METHOD: Put all grapes in a suitable vessel and crush them,

> making sure each grape is crushed. Measure as near as you can or judge as accurately as possible the amount of pulp you have and to each gallon allow one Campden tablet or four grains of sodium metabisulphite. Dissolve this in an eggcupful of warm water and stir into the pulp and leave for☐ twenty-four hours.
> After this, give the mixture a thorough mixing and churning and then add the yeast. The mixture should then be left to ferment for five days.
> Following this, the pulp should be strained through a strong coarse cloth to prevent bursting and wrung out as dry as you can. The liquor should then be put
> into jars and fermented the same ways as other wines.

A good plan when doing this is to mix a quart of water with grape pulp and to crush this well to get as much from the skins as you can. If you do this, you must add one pound of sugar and dissolve it by warming the juice just enough for

this purpose. This thinner juice may be mixed with the rest
but before the better quality juice is put into jars.

Where grapes only are used with water (as suggested above) it
must be borne in mind that to get enough alcohol for a stable
wine we must have between two and two and a half pounds of
sugar to the gallon. Juice crushed from grapes rarely
contains this much, therefore it would be wise to add one
pound when the fruit is crushed and before the juice is put
into jars. If the wine turns out dry, it may be sweetened.

We may use a hydrometer to find the sugar content so that we
know how much to add to give the amount of alcohol we need,
but this is not for beginners without previous experiences in
this sort of thing. The better plan is to follow my
suggestions above, and if the wine is dry to sweeten it and
then preserve it with Campden tablets or metabisulphite as
directed in chapter six.

Since the color comes from the skins, if we want a red wine
from black grapes we ferment the skins as directed earlier in
this chapter. A white wine from black grapes is made by
crushing the grapes and pressing out the juice and fermenting
the juice only. The difference in the process already
described is that instead of fermenting the skin for five

days, the juice is pressed out after it has been allowed to
soak for twenty-four hours.

If you happen to be making some of the fruit wine such as
elderberry, plum, blackberry or damson, at the same time as
making grape wine, it would be a good idea to put the
strained fruit pulp which would otherwise be discarded into
the 'must' of the other fruit and let it ferment there. But

do not alter the fermentation times of the other recipe that
you are using for the other fruit.

If an abundance of grapes is not available the following
recipes will be found especially valuable. The methods to
use are those given for making the various fresh fruit wines
in chapter two. Bear in mind that the grapes must be
fermented when a red wine is required whilst the juice only
is fermented when a white wine is required. This applies to
black grapes, of course; you can do anything you like with
those called amber or the green ones.

92. WINES FROM GRAPES:
    RECIPE 1

    9 to 12 lb. grapes, 2 lb. raisins, 2 qts water, -lb.
    sugar, port yeast or burgundy yeast.

RECIPE 2

8 to 10 lb. grapes, 2 lb. prunes, 2 qts. water, 2 lb.
sugar, port or burgundy yeast.

RECIPE 3

10 lb. black grapes, 1 lb. prunes, 2 lb. raisins, 1 1/2
lb. sugar, 4 qts. water, port or burgundy yeast.

RECIPE 4

10 lb. grapes, 2 lb. elderberries, 4 pts water, 2 lb.
sugar, port or burgundy yeast.

RECIPE 5

8 lb. grapes, 6 lb. damsons or red plums, 2 lb. sugar, 2
qts. water, port or burgundy yeast.

NOTE: Owing to the difficulty in getting juice from plums
and damsons, the pulp must be fermented for a time,
so it is not practicable to ferment the juice only
in this recipe.

RECIPE 6

8 to 10 lb. grapes, 2 lb. blackberries, 4 pts. water,
port or burgundy yeast, 2 lb. sugar.

NOTE: Nutrient is not needed because the grape juice
provides sufficient.

LIQUEURS

In my grandmother's day brandy cost about fifty cents a
bottle (now we know what is meant by "the good old days") and
her recipes call for gallons of the stuff as casually as
today's call for one measly bottle.

Nevertheless, one bottle of gin, whisky or brandy will give
two bottles of the finished product with a high precentage of
alcohol to half the cost of the commercial product.

Before going on to the recipes, let me explain that a
homemade wine usually has alcohol content of fourteen percent
by volume (approximately 24 proof). Such a wine will keep

well because this amount of alcohol is usually high enough to
destroy souring yeast and the bacteria which causes
vinegariness immediately when it comes in contact with them.
Thus it will be seen that a nice precentage of alcohol acts
as its own preservative.

The alcohol content of commercial wines rarely exceeds twenty
percent by volume (approximately 35 proof); more often they
range between fourteen percent by volume (approximately 24
proof) and nineteen percent (approximately 33 proof), which
is a high percentage of alcohol. Clearly, then, we could
very well dilute the 70 proof gin (forty percent by volume)

to 35 proof (twenty percent by volume) by making one bottle
into two bottles and still have a very strong sloe gin.

Whisky and rum could be similarly treated, while brandy might
well be diluted even more owing to its higher spirit content.
Bear in mind that it would be unwise to reduce the proof too
below 30. The best plan to start with is to make one bottle
into two as the recipes advise or make half a bottle into a
whole bottle by using half of everything in the recipes.

You could make three or four bottles from one bottle of the
spirit if you were proposing to use it up fairly quickly,

such as at a party or over the three day Christmas.

Naturally, we shall be diluting the flavors of the spirits we
are using, but we shall be adding the flavors of our choice
to counter-balance this. In any case, the commercial spirits
mentioned above are rarely drunk meat. Whisky is usually
diluted with water (which in my opinion is nigh on a crime)
or ginger of soda, while run is often diluted with peppermint
or orange cordial. Gin is usually diluted with lemon or

orange cordial to make the popular gin and orange, etc. And
in most cases the spirit is diluted to one-third of its
volume. Therefore, the proof spirit content of the whisky
and soda or gin and orange served over the bar has been
reduced to about 23 proof. the sloe gin we shall be making
with these recipes will be 35 proof while the cherry brandy
will be 40 proof. Bear in this in mind while drinking them
other wise you will finish up under the table in doublequick
time.

If you happen to have some home-made sloe wine, damson wine,
orange wine, cherry wine or some other sort of home-made
wine, you may employ one bottle of the spirits to make more
than two bottles of cherry brandy, sloe gin or whichever you
have in mind. This point is covered fully further on in this chapter.

The following recipes produces wines which are neither sweet
nor dry; if you like a slightly sweet wine increase the
amount of sugar by half that given in the recipes. On the
other hand, if you like wines drier than average reduce the
amount of sugar by half.

In the recipes called liqueurs, the amount of sugar should
remain as in the recipes.

NOTE: As we shall be using bottles as our means of measuring
our materials, bear in mind that a bottle is a bottle

and half a bottle is half a bottle. A bottle-the

recognized standard wine bottle or the bottles
containing spirits-hold five gills; this is one gill more
than a pint. Many bottles containing imported
wines hold one pint. Because we shall be making
exactly two bottles from on bottle of the spirit we are
using, be sure to at the second bottle you use holds
the same amount as the bottle of spirit you are using.
If you are using White Horse whisky or Booth's gin, try
to use a similar second bottle.

93. CHERRY BRANDY LIQUEUR:

1 1/2 lb. black cherries, 8 oz. white sugar, 1 bottle
brandy, 8 blanched almonds (these are usually added, but
personal tastes must decide.)
Wash the cherries and let the drain. Pour the brandy
into a four-pound Kilner jar (these are best), then stone
and halve the cherries carefully and add them to the
brandy. Add the almonds if you like them.
Screw down tightly and put in a cool, preferably dark,
place for six to eight weeks. Give the jar a good
shaking twice a week.
Strain and squeeze and put the liquid into a smaller jar
then put away as before and leave to clear. Then pour or
siphon into two wine bottles-putting exactly half into
each. Then boil the sugar in one pint of water for two
minutes. When this is cool, fill the bottles to within
one inch of where the cork will reach. Shake well to
ensure thorough mixing. Seal and keep for one month.

94. DAMSON GIN:

1 lb. damsons, 3 oz. sugar, 1 bottle gin.
Wash, dry, stone and halve the damsons carefully and put
them in a four-pound Kilner jar. Sprinkle the sugar over
them and then pour in the gin.
Screw down tightly and leave in a cool dark place for
three months (or two months if you are in a hurry to use
the product), giving a good shaking once or twice a week.
Strain and squeeze and put the strained damson gin into a
smaller jar, screw down again and put it away to clear.
Then pour carefully (or siphon) the clear gin off the
deposit putting exactly half into two bottles. Then fill
the bottles to within one inch of where the corks will
reach with boiled water that has cooled naturally. Cork
hard, seal and keep for one month.

95. SLOE GIN:

1 lb. sloes, 5 oz. sugar, 1 bottle gin.
Wash the sloes and let them drain. Prick the sloes all

over with a silver, or stainless-steel fork or large
darning needle and put them in a four-pound Kilner jar.
Sprinkle the sugar over them and then pour in the gin.
Screw down tightly and put in a cool dark place for six
weeks. give the gar a good shaking once a week.
Strain and squeeze and put the strained sloe gin into a
smaller jar, screw down tightly again and put away until
clear.

Pour carefully (or siphon) the clear sloe gin off the
deposit and put exactly half into each of two bottles.
Fill the bottles to within one inch of where the corks
will reach with boiled water that has cooled naturally.

Mix well by shaking, cork seal and keep for one month.

96. ORANGE WHISKY:

4 oranges, 2 lemons, 2 seville oranges (or an extra
ordinary orange and lemon), 4 oz. sugar, 1 bottle whisky.
Peel the fruits and remove all the white pith. Crush
well and put the pulp in a four pound Kilner jar. Grate
the rind of one orange (not a seville), avoiding any
white pith, and add this to the pulp. Sprinkle in the
sugar and pour on the whisky. Screw down tightly and put
the jar in a cool dark place for a week-giving it a shake
every day.
Strain into another jar and squeeze the screw down again
tightly. then put it away to clear.
Pour or siphon the clear whisky into bottles, putting
exactly half into each. Then fill the bottles to within
an inch of where the corks will reach with boiled water
that has cooled naturally. Cork hark, seal and keep for
at least two months.

97. ORANGE GIN:

6 oranges, 1 lemon, 2 seville oranges (or an extra
ordinary orange and lemon), 5 oz. sugar, 1 bottle gin.
Proceed as for orange whisky.

98. FRUIT LIQUEURS:

There is no need to give separate recipes for each fruit
because the same process may be used for all suitable
fresh fruit of your choice. The following lists the most
suitable fruits for liqueur-making and the amounts given
usually produce sufficient flavour-though not enough
juice-to make two bottles of liqueur when using one
bottle of brandy. If not enough juice is produced from
the amounts of fruit given, make up the amount required
with boiled water, bearing in mind that half a pound of
sugar occupies the space of a quarter-pint while one

pound occupies half a pint space and so on.

All these liqueurs will have a spirit content of 40 proof-which, as we have seen, is a high spirit content.

As we shall be using spirit of 80 proof, we could make two and a half bottles by using a little more juice, a little more water and an ounce or two more sugar and still have a product of 32 proof-which is a nice spirit content.

If at party time economy is essential, three or even four bottles of a liqueur-type wine could be made from one bottle of brandy or, say, cherry brandy, sloe gin or whatever you have in mind, if it were intended to use them up over a weekend or over a three day Christmas. See making liqueurs from wines and making liqueurs from extracts.

One bottle of liqueur may be made by using exactly half the amounts listed below and a little water.

FRESH FRUIT	QUANTITY (lb.)	SUGAR (oz.)	BRANDY
Blackcurrants	1	4	1 bottle
Redcurrants	1 1/2	5	1 bottle
Strawberries	1 1/2	3	1 bottle
Cherries	2	4	1 bottle
Raspberries	1	5	1 bottle
Loganberries	1	4	1 bottle
Blackberries	1	5	1 bottle

Crush the fruit by hand, put in a basin and keep in a very warm place for twelve hours, well covered. Strain carefully through several thicknesses of fine muslin or other suitable material. Allow to drain rather than squeeze.

Put the strained juice into a bottle of the same size as the brandy bottle and fill with boiled water that has been allowed to cool. Mix well by shaking, cork hard and put in a cool place for one hour. By this time a deposit will have formed. Pour the clear juice off this deposit, leaving a little juice rather than allowing any deposit through. The deposit may cause permanent cloudiness if boiled with the clear juice.

Put the clear juice in a small unchipped enamel saucepan with sugar and boil gently for two minutes. When cool put exactly

half into two bottles of the same size as the brandy bottle and then fill up with brandy. Add a few drops of boiled

water if the liquid does not reach to within one inch of
where the corks will reach. Then cork hard and seal after

giving a good shaking to ensure thorough mixing and keep for
a month at least. If a film of deposit forms at the bottom
of the bottles, decant before serving.

LIQUEURS AND PARTY SPECIALS
(FROM HOME-MADE WINES)

Most of us have stocks of home-made wine and, at party time
or at Christmas, we often wonder how we can turn them into
'party specials' and do so inexpensively. The main question
always is: How much spirit to add to get a given percentage
of alcohol.

Firstly, and in the ordinary way, a well-made wine will not
need doctoring of this sort because if fermentation was
satisfactory the alcohol content will be in the region of
fourteen percent by volume (24 to 26 proof). This is the
alcohol content of most commercial wines; indeed, some are
lower in alcohol than this while others are, of course,
higher.

Come party time the question is often one of economy-how to
make that one bottle of Scotch, or gin or rum, go farther
without the economy being noticeable. As already mentioned,
spirits are hardly drunk meat; additions of some sort are
usually employed, such as ginger, orange or lemon cordial,
and these reduce the alcohol content to about a quarter. For
those who want to experiment a bit on their own accord, the
table shows the relation between alcohol by volume and proof
spirit, and the range covered by this allows for the limits
within which they will be working.

Those not wishing to start from scratch will find the
following guidance useful.

Let me begin with whisky, gin or rum of 70 proof. Wines made
with the following fruits are ideal for mixing with gin,

either sweetened or unsweetened-damson, sloe, lemon, orange.

We have a bottle of one or the other of these wines and a
bottle of gin handy. The gin contains forty percent alcohol
by volume and a bottle of wine fourteen percent. Mix the two
and you have (for the sake of simplicity) twice as much of
both. Therefore you have twenty percent by volume (the gin)

and seven percent by volume (the wine), total of twenty-seven
percent by volume.

To make it simpler:
The gin 40 percent by volume
The wine 14 percent by volume
        54 percent

But because the volume (amount) has been doubled, the alcohol
content has been reduced by half-twenty seven percent by
volume. As we can get fifty-four percent of alcohol in this
way we could use two bottles of wine and one of gin and get
three bottles of a product containing eighteen percent.

NOTE: It is important to understand that when two bottles of
     wine at 14% of alcohol are put together you have twice
     as much wine still at 14%. But when you do this for
     the purpose of fortifying, the alcohol in each bottle
     must be accounted for. Therefore, three bottles of
     wine each containing 14% equals 42%, plus one bottle of
     gin at 40% = 82%. Divide this figure by the number of
     resulting bottles-in this case four bottles-and each

     will contain just over 20%.

Going further-5 bottles at 14% = 70%
          1 bottle gin at   40%

                 Total 110%

In this case six bottles result, therefore 110 divided by 6 =
18% approximately. The same would apply when whisky or rum
are used.

Wines more suitable for mixing with whisky are:
Root wines (not beetroot).
Root wines made with cereals such as wheat, and with raisins,
or both, or with wheat or raisins alone added.
Grain wines -- those made mainly with wheat or maize, etc.
Orange.

Dandelion.

Wines more suitable for mixing with rum:
Root wines with a rather higher than average acid content.
Other more acid wines such as rhubarb.
Orange.
Lemon.

Grapefruit.

Wines more suitable for mixing with port and other high
alcohol red wines:

Elderberry and all of the red wines whether made from one
fruit or a mixture of fruits, or mixtures of fruits and

grains such as wheat or maize.
White wines or the paler-color ones made from such fruits as
raisins, raspberries, loganberries, red or white currants,
etc., may be mixed with the higher-alcohol white 'ports' or
high-alcohol white wines.

NOTE: Owing to the lower alcohol content of port as compared
with spirits, the mixing should be confined to one

bottle of wine to the bottle of port if they are
required for keeping. Two to one mixing may be
practiced where it is intended to use up the product

within, say, three or four days.

WINES FOR THE LADIES

(Preserved, Sweet or Dry Wines of Low Alcohol Content)

It is mostly men who want their wines to be knock-out drops
and usually they take care to get them as strong as possible.
But a high percentage of alcohol is not everything.
Many-indeed, I would say most-continental wines are in the
region of eight to eleven percent of alcohol. Ours, made
with the recipes in this book, will be a good deal stronger
than this as has already been explained. It is the ladies
who like the milder-flavored, low-alcohol, dry to medium-dry
or medium-dry to sweet wines, so let me explain how any
recipe here may be quite easily turned into a 'wine for the
ladies'.

Mentioned in earlier chapters is the fact that a good
percentage of alcohol ensures that wines keep well, and that
the lower-alcohol wines -- those under twelve percent-might
begin ferment again at any time. This is because a stray
yeast spore, either left in the wine or one reaching it at
some later stage, will begin to reproduce and live on any
sugar present. Only the very driest of low-alcohol wines
will keep and these must be so dry that no unfermented sugar
remains at all.

However, not everybody likes bone-dry wines; most people
prefer them medium dry to medium sweet or even sweet.

The wines made with the recipes in this book will keep well
provided the maximum alcohol has been reached, an if all
directions have been followed this will have been achieved.
they will keep because they contain enough alcohol to destroy
any yeast or bacteria that may reach them.

Our aim when making low-alcohol wines is to add just enough
sugar to make the amount of alcohol required and to allow the
wine to ferment right out, and this will do of its own

accord. the wine will be dry if less than two and a quarter
pounds of sugar are used for one gallon.

Now take a look at the short table. This shows the amount of
sugar needed to produce the amount of alcohol required in one
gallon of wine; if two gallons are being made the amount of
sugar required would have to be doubled.

Let us suppose we have decided on making a wine of ten
percent of alcohol: The amount of sugar to add is
approximately one pound fourteen ounces per gallon.

Very well then, take any recipe in this book (but not those
containing dried fruit as these contain quite a lot of sugar)
and instead of using the amount of sugar given in that
recipe, use one pound and fourteen ounces instead.

As already mentioned, the resulting wine will be bone dry-to
dry even for those fond of the drier wines. To reduce this
dryness we may sweeten to taste either by adding dissolved
invert sugar (which dissolves quite readily) or by dissolving
household sugar in some of the wine in the following manner.

Care must be taken here to ensure that the wine does not come
into contact with metals. One pint of wine from one gallon

will do. Put this into a china jug or similar vessel and
stand this in a saucepan of water. Add, say, one teaspoonful
of sugar for each bottle (one per gallon, six bottles) and
warm the water until the sugar in the wine is dissolved. Mix
this with the bulk and sample. If this is not quite sweet
enough, you will know that the may be repeated. If you are
using invert sugar, the sugar itself may be dissolved in an
enamel sauce pan and the resulting syrup stirred into the
wine.

Very well, we now have a low-alcohol wine with sugar in it.
To prevent it fermenting or some later date we may preserve
it without harming it in any way.

Here again, Campden tablets play their part, but if the wine
is crystal clear, Campden tablets might cloud it slightly.
This should settle our, but it would mean that rebottling
might be necessary when this had happened. It is better
therefore to use four grains of potassium metabisulphite in

place of one Campden tablet. This should be enough to preserve one gallon of wine.

Crush the bisulphite crystals, and dissolve them in a little warmed wine and stir this into the bulk immediately after sweetening. Make sure the crystals are quite dissolved. I have written that one Campden tablet (or four grains of bisulpite crystals) should preserve a gallon of wine-and so it should, but under exceptional circumstances it might not. One more tablet (or four more grains of bisulphite crystals) may be added without harmful effects, except that it might give just a hint of flavour to the most delicately flavored wines-through it will not affect those with a good all-round flavor. Fortunately, there is a simple test that we may

carry out to decide whether a second tablet is needed or not.

First, pour a little of the treated wine into a wine-glass and bung down the remainder. cover the glass with a small piece of cloth and leave in a warm room (not a hot place), overnight or for eight to twelve hours. Note carefully the color when setting it out again the following morning (or compare this sample with a sample freshly drawn from the bulk). If darkening of the sample left overnight has occurred, then an extra tablet is needed. If darkening has not occurred, one tablet (four grains metabisulphite) has done the job, and you have a low-alcohol wine of required dryness or sweetness that will keep well.

Up to 450 parts SO2 are allowed by law in 1,000,000 parts wine, and this is represented by approximately eight Campden tablets (or thirty-two grains potassium metabisulphite). Two tablets (eight grains) represents just over one hundred parts per million; so it will be seen that we are not, after all,

using very much.

Dry wines finish fermenting sooner than wines of a higher alcoholic content because there is less sugar to be fermented out.

This preserving of wines may be carried out with all wines if you wish, whether they be high-alcohol wines or not.

SUGAR		POTENTIALALCOHOL
lb.	oz.	per cent
1	4	7.6
1	8	9.2
1	14	10.8
2	0	12.3

The above figures refer to the use of household sugar. If
invert sugar is being used, it must be borne in mind that
this contains some moisture, so that for every pound of

household sugar one must use use one and a quarter pounds of
invert sugar. So that mistakes do not occur, I have included
the amounts of each sugar to use so that you may choose for
yourself which to use and know how much of either-not both.

Invert sugar is usually supplied in tins containing seven
pounds or in blocks by whatever weight is ordered. If
weighing this proves awkward, dissolve it and measure it by
the pint, bearing in mind that one pint represents two pounds
of sugar.

WINE FROM EXTRACTS

41. CHERRY BRANDY WINE:

6 bottles of cherry brandy extract, 3 lb. sugar (or 3 3/4
invert), 1 gal. water, yeast and nutrient.
Boil one-third of the sugar in half a gallon of water for
two minutes, allow to cool and pour into the gallon jar.
Then add the extract, yeast and nutrient.
Cover as directed of fit fermentation lock and ferment in
a warm place for ten days. Then boil another third of
the sugar in a further quart of water for two minutes and
when cool add this to the rest. Cover again as before or
refit the lock and continue to ferment in a warm place
for a further fourteen days.
After this, boil the rest of the sugar in the remaining
quart of water as before and when cool add the the rest.
Cover again or refit the lock and leave in a cool place
until all fermentation has ceased.

42. VERMOUTH (ITALIAN):

6 bottles of Italian Vermouth extract, 3 lb. sugar (or 3
3/4 lb. invert), yeast and nutrient.
Boil one-third of the sugar in a half-gallon of water for
two minutes. Allow to cool and pour into a gallon jar.
Then add the extract, yeast and nutrient.
Cover as directed or fit fermentation lock and ferment in
a warm place for ten days. The boil another one-third of
the sugar in a further quart of water and when this is
cool add it to the rest. Cover again or refit the lock
and continue to ferment in a warm place for a further
fourteen days. After this, boil the remaining sugar in
the remaining quart of water as before, when add to the
rest. Cover again or refit the lock and leave in a warm

place until all fermentation has ceased.

43. VERMOUTH (FRENCH):

6 bottles of French Vermouth extract, 3 1/4 lb. sugar (or
4 lb. invert), 1 gal. water, yeast nutrient.
Boil one-third of the sugar in half a gallon of water for
two minutes and when cool pour into a gallon jar. Then
add the extract, yeast and nutrient.
Cover as directed or fit fermentation lock and ferment in
a warm place for ten days. Then boil another one-one
third of the sugar in a quart of water for two minutes
and when cool add this to the rest. Allow to ferment in
a warm place for a further fourteen days.
After this, boil the remaining water and sugar as before
and when cool add to the rest.
Cover again or refit the lock and continue to ferment in
a warm place until all fermentation has ceased.

44. CREAM OF APRICOT WINE:

5 bottles of apricot extract, 3 lb. sugar, (or 3 3/4 lb.
invert), 1 gal. water, yeast and nutrient.
Boil one-third of the sugar in half a gallon of water for
two minutes, allow to cool and pour into a gallon jar.
Then add the extract, yeast and nutrient.
Cover as directed or fit fermentation lock and ferment in
a warm place for ten days. The boil another third of the
sugar in a quart of the water for two minutes and when
this is cool add it to the rest. Cover again as directed
or refit fermentation lock and continue to ferment in a
warm place for a further fourteen days.
After this, boil the rest of the sugar in the remaining
water as before and when cool add to the rest. Cover
again or refit lock and continue to ferment in a warm
place until all fermentation has ceased.

45. CREAM OF PEACH WINE:

6 bottles of cream of peach, 3 lb. sugar (or 3 3/4 lb.
invert), 1 gal. water, yeast and nutrient.
Boil one-third of the sugar in half-gallon of water for
two minutes and when cool pour into a gallon-size glass
jar. Then add the extract, yeast and nutrient.
Cover as directed or fit fermentation lock and ferment in
a warm place for ten days.
Then boil another one-third of the sugar in a quart or
water and when cool add this to the rest. Cover again as
directed or refit the lock and continue to ferment in a
warm place for a further fourteen days.
After this, boil the rest of the sugar in the remaining

water as before and when cool add to the rest. Cover
again as directed or refit the lock and continue to
ferment in a warm place until all fermentation has
ceased.

46. SLOE GIN WINE:

6 bottles of sloe gin extract, 3 lb. sugar (or 3 3/4 lb.
invert), 1 gal. water, yeast and nutrient.
Boil one third of the sugar in a half gallon of water for
two minutes and when cool pour into a gallon jar. Then
add the extract, yeast and nutrient.
Cover as directed or fit fermentation lock and ferment in
a warm place for ten days. Then boil another one-third
of the sugar in a quart of water as be fore and when this
is cool add to the rest. Cover again or refit lock and
continue to ferment in a warm place for a further
fourteen days.
Then boil the rest of the sugar in the remaining water as
before and then cool add to the rest. Cover again refit
the lock and continue to ferment in a warm place until
all fermentation has ceased.

47. RATAFIA WINE:

6 bottles of Ratafia extract, 3 lb. sugar (or 3 3/4 lb.
invert), 1 gal. water, yeast and nutrient.
Boil one-third of the sugar in a half gallon of water for
two minutes and when cool pour into a gallon glass jar.
Then add the extract, yeast and nutrient.
Cover as directed or fit fermentation lock and ferment in
a warm place for ten days. The boil another one-third of
the sugar in a quart of water as before and when this is
cool add it to the rest. Cover again or refit lock and
continue to ferment in a warm place for a further
fourteen days.
After this, boil the rest of the sugar in the remaining
water as before and when cool add to the rest.
Cover again as directed or fit fermentation lock and
continue to ferment in a warm place until all
fermentation has ceased.

48. KIRSCH WINE:

6 bottles of Kirsch extract, 3 lb. sugar (or 3 3/4 lb.
invert), 1 gal. water, yeast and nutrient.
Boil one-third of the sugar in half a gallon of water for
two minutes and when cool pour into a gallon glass jar.
Then add the extract, yeast and nutrient.
Cover as directed or fit fermentation lock and ferment in
a warm place for ten days.

Then boil another one-third of the sugar in a quart of water as before and when this is cool add it to the rest. Cover as directed or refit lock and continue to ferment in a warm place for a further fourteen days.

After this, boil the remaining sugar in the rest of the water as before and when cool add to the rest. Cover again as directed or refit the lock and continue to ferment in a warm place until all fermentation has ceased.

49. MIRABELLE WINE:

6 bottles of Mirabelle extract, 3 lb. sugar (or 3 3/4 lb. invert), 1 gal. water, yeast and nutrient.
Boil one-third of the sugar in a half gallon of water for two minutes and when cool pour into a gallon glass jar. Then add the extract, yeast and nutrient.
Cover as directed or fit fermentation lock and ferment in a warm place for ten days. The boil another one-third of the sugar in a quart of water as before and when it is cool add to the rest. Cover again or refit the lock and ferment in a warm place for another fourteen days.
After this, boil the remaining sugar in the rest of the water as before and when cool add to the rest.
Cover again as directed or refit the lock and continue to ferment in a warm place until all fermentation has ceased.

50. PRUNELLE WINE:

6 bottles of Prunelle extract, 3 lb. sugar, (or 3 3/4 invert), 1 gal. water, yeast and nutrient.
Boil one-third of the sugar in half a gallon of water for two minutes and when cool pour into a gallon jar. Then add the extract, yeast and nutrient.
Cover as directed or fit fermentation lock and ferment in a warm place for ten days. Then boil another one-third of the sugar in a quart of water as before and when this is cool add it to the rest. Cover again or refit the lock and continue to ferment in a warm place for a further fourteen days.
After this, boil the remaining sugar in the rest of the water as before and when cool add to the rest.
Cover again or refit the lock and continue to ferment in a warm place until all fermentation has ceased.

51. MARASQUIN WINE:

6 bottles of Marassquin extract, 3 lb. sugar (or 3 3/4 lb. invert), 1 gal. water, yeast and nutrient.
Boil one-third of sugar in a half gallon of water for two

minutes and when cool pour into gallon glass jar. Then
pour in the extract, yeast and nutrient.

Cover as directed or fit fermentation lock and ferment in
a warm place for ten days. Then boil another one-third
of the sugar in a quart of water for two minutes and when
cool add this to the rest. Cover again or refit lock and
continue to ferment in a warm place for another fourteen
days.
After this, boil the remaining sugar in the rest of the
water as before and when cool add to the rest. Cover
again or refit the lock and continue to ferment in a warm
place until all fermentation has ceased.

52. MANDARINE WINE:

6 bottles of Mandarine extract, 3 lb. sugar (or 3 3/4 lb.
invert), a gal. water, yeast and nutrient.
Boil one-third of sugar in a gallon of water for two
minutes and when cool pour into a gallon glass jar. Then
add the extract, yeast and nutrient.
Cover as directed or fit fermentation lock and ferment in
a warm place for ten days. Then boil another one-third
of the sugar in a quart of water as before and when cool
add this to the rest. cover again or refit lock and
continue to ferment in a warm place for a further
fourteen days.
After this, boil the remaining sugar in the rest of the
water as before and when cool add to the rest.
Cover again or refit the lock and continue to ferment in
a warm place until all fermentation has ceased.

53. GREEN CONVENT WINE:

5 bottles of Green Convent extract, 3 lb. sugar (or 3 3/4
lb. invert), 1 gal. water, yeast and nutrient.
Boil one-third of the sugar in half a gallon of water for
two minutes and when cool pour into a gallon glass jar.
Then add the extract, yeast and nutrient. Cover as
directed or fit fermentation lock and ferment in a warm
place for ten days. Then boil another one-third of the
sugar in a quart of water as before and when cool add
this to the rest. Cover again and continue to ferment
for another fourteen days.
After this, boil the remaining sugar in the rest of the
water as before and when cool add to the rest. Cover
again and continue to ferment until all fermentation has
ceased.

54. YELLOW CONVENT WINE:

5 bottles of Yellow Convent extract, 3 lb. sugar (or 3

3/4 lb. invert), 1 gal. water, yeast and nutrient.
Boil one-third of the sugar in half a gallon of water for
two minutes and when cool pour into a gallon glass jar.
Then pour in the extract, yeast and nutrient.
Cover and ferment for ten days. Then boil another
one-third of the sugar and when cool add it to the rest.
Cover again and continue to ferment in a warm place for
another fourteen days.
Then boil the remaining sugar in the rest of the water as
before and when cool add to the rest. Cover again and
ferment in a warm place until all fermentation has
ceased.

55. REVERENDINE WINE:

6 bottles of Reverendine extract, 3 lb. sugar (or 3 3/4
lb. invert), 1 gal. water, yeast nutrient.
Boil one-third of the sugar in half a gallon of water for
two minutes and when cool pour into a gallon glass jar.
Then pour in the extract, yeast and nutrient.
Cover and ferment in a warm place for ten days. Then
boil another one-third of the sugar as before and when
cool add it to the rest.
Cover again and continue to ferment in a warm place for a
further fourteen days.□
After this, boil the remaining sugar in the rest of the
water as before and when cool add it to the rest. Cover
again and continue to ferment in a warm place until all
fermentation has ceased.

56. RED CURACAO WINE:

6 bottles of Red Curacao extract, 3 lb. sugar, (or 3 3/4
lb. invert), 1 gal. water, yeast and nutrient.
Boil one-third of the sugar in half a gallon of water for
two minutes and when cool pour into a glass jar. Then
add the extract, yeast and nutrient.
Cover and ferment in a warm place for ten days. Then
boil another one-third of the sugar as before and when
cool add it to the rest. Cover again and ferment in a
warm place for another fourteen days.
After this, boil the remaining sugar in the rest of the
water as before and when cool add it to the rest. Cover
again and continue to ferment until all fermentation has
ceased.

57. WHITE CURACAO WINE:

6 bottles of White Curacao extract, 3 lb. sugar (or 3 3/4
lb. invert) 1 gal. water, yeast and nutrient.
Boil one-third of the sugar in half a gallon of water and

when this is cool pour into a gallon glass jar. then
pour in the extract, and add the yeast and nutrient.
Cover the jar and ferment in a warm place for ten days.
Then boil another one-third of the sugar in a quart of
water as before and when cool add to the rest. Cover
again and continue to ferment for another fourteen days.
After this, boil the remaining sugar in the rest of the
water as before and when cool add to the rest. Cover
again and ferment in a warm place until all fermentation
has ceased.

58. KUMMEL WINE:

6 bottles of Kummel extract, 3 lb. sugar (or 3 3/4 lb.
invert), 1 gal. water, yeast and nutrient.
Boil one-third of the sugar in half a gallon of water for
two minutes and when cool pour into a gallon glass
bottle. Then add the extract, yeast and nutrient.
Cover and fermentation for ten days. Then boil another
one-third of the sugar in a quart of water as before and
when this is cool add it to the rest.
Cover again and ferment in a warm place for another
fourteen days. After this, boil the remaining sugar in
the rest of the water as before and when cool add it to
the rest. Cover again and continue to ferment in a warm
place until all fermentation has ceased.

59. DANZIG WINE:

6 bottles of Danzig extract, 3 lb. sugar (or 3 3/4 lb.
invert), 1 gal. water, yeast and nutrient.
Boil one-third of the sugar in half a gallon of water for
two minutes and when cool pour into a gallon glass jar.
Then pour in the extract, yeast and nutrient.
Cover and ferment in a warm place for ten days. Then
boil another one-third of the sugar in a quart of water
as before and when cool add this to the rest. Cover
again and continue to ferment in a warm place for another
fourteen days.
After this, boil the remaining sugar in the rest of the
water as before and when it is cool add it to the rest.
Cover again and ferment in a warm place until all
fermentation has ceased.

60. EAU-DE-VIE WINE:

6 bottles of extract of Eau-de-Vie, 3 lb. sugar (or 3 3/4
lb. invert), 1 gal. water, yeast and nutrient.
Boil one-third of the sugar in half a gallon of water for
two minutes and when cool pour into a gallon glass jar.
Then add extract, yeast and nutrient.

Cover as directed and ferment in a warm place for ten
days. Then boil another one-third of the sugar in a
quart of water as before and when cool add this to the
rest. Cover again and ferment in a warm place for
another fourteen days. After this, boil the remaining
sugar in the rest of the water as before and when cool
add to the rest.
Cover again as directed and continue to ferment in a warm
place until all fermentation has ceased.

APPENDIX

SUGGESTIONS FOR READERS WHO HAVE DIFFICULTY OBTAINING
SOME OF THE SUPPLIES MENTIONED.

INVERT SUGAR   -- This can be made at home by the reader
                if he has difficulty obtaining same: Put
                8 lb. of ordinary household sugar (white
                sugar) in a suitable pan with 2 pints of
                water and 1/2 ounce of citric acid
                (obtainable in drug stores), or use the
                juice of four lemons. Bring slowly to a
                boil, stirring all the time so that all
                sugar dissolves.

                When all sugar is dissolved, allow to
                boil for half an hour very gently
                without stirring -- or stirring only
                occasionally. Allow this to cool
                somewhat and then make up to exactly 1
                gallon by adding boiled water.
                You now have INVERT SUGAR-the inversion
                being caused by the acid. To measure,
                use 1 pint to each lb. sugar called for
                in the recipe -- 1 pint is equal to 1
                lb. sugar.
                Store in suitable jars, tightly corked.
YEAST NUTRIENTS   -- These are blends of chemicals which
                stimulate yeast reproduction, thereby
                helping the yeast to make as much
                alcohol as it is capable of making.
                There are no actual substitutes.,
CAMPDEN TABLETS   -- A substitute is given in the book. Four
                grains of sodium metabisulphite is
                equivalent to one Campden tablet. Your
                druggist will probably think four grains
                too small an order, so ask him for an

order of, say, ten packs of four grains
each, and use one four-grain pack for
each Campden tablet called for in the
recipe. Do not buy by the ounce and try
to measure four grains yourself.

RIBENA   -- If you cannot obtain this, try to
substitute black-currant syrup instead.
However, it is best to use RIBENA
proper.

CONTAINERS   -- Good quality tin or stainless steel
containers may be used quite safely, but
do not use vessels specifically not
recommended by the author, and do not
use galvanized containers.

NOW MAKE SOME WINE!!!